DOWN THE YORKSHIRE PAN

A nostalgic look back to the Good Old Days in North Yorkshire

Dulcie Lewis

COUNTRYSIDE BOOKS

NEWBURY, BERKSHIRE

COUNTRYSIDE BOOKS
3 Catherine Road
Newbury, Berkshire

To view our complete range of books,
please visit us at
www.countrysidebooks.co.uk

ISBN 1 85306 645 1

Produced through MRM Associates Ltd., Reading
Printed by J. W. Arrowsmith Ltd., Bristol

Contents

— ❧ —

Foreword

— ❦ —

Soon after coming to live in North Yorkshire I was introduced to someone in Leyburn market square as, 'This is Dulcie Lewis – she gives talks on the lavatory.' What conflicting images this must have conjured up for the poor lady. However, it is indeed true as for many years now I have tried to entertain any group that would care to listen with various humorous topics. The talk in greatest demand is 'Down the Pan' – a history of the bath and the lavatory. There is a desire for enlightenment on this fragrant topic and over the years my knowledge of these two bodily functions has become extensive. A dubious attainment you may think; but none the less an achievement of some kind.

Married to a Yorkshireman who on his retirement wanted to return to his roots, it seemed on the whole a good idea to come with him. Settling into my new home in Wensleydale I naturally wished to discover as much as possible about this beautiful area. The history, the people, the customs and, given my particular interests, where better to start than with their hygiene habits. The people of North Yorkshire have nothing to be ashamed of when it comes to these matters: they stand up well to scrutiny.

The size of this book dictates that my researches are limited to the north of this large and diverse county – the Dales in particular, with a few sorties east of the A1 for some interesting sightings. I do not attempt to reveal all behind the bathroom and lavatory door but will gently peep round it at what used to go on. So how did the people of North Yorkshire keep themselves clean, decent and healthy? These are not mere scatological musings but social history of the kind to affect us all.

So dear Reader, let us go forth together and flush out the truth, turning on the taps of history and memories to bathe in the waters of Cleanliness and Godliness.

Dulcie Lewis

Murky Waters

——— ✣ ———

'Let thy fingers be clean. Thou must not put thy fingers into thine ears, or thy hands on the head.' A 15th century 'Boke of Curtasye'.

We must now sink back into history for a short soak to see what went before us. We have always had an ambivalent attitude towards water. Whilst recognising that water is necessary for life, we have not until recently wanted to wallow in the stuff. Put succinctly: to defecate is vital for our wellbeing; to bathe is not. Wherever water has to be carried any distance by hand, bathing is strictly limited.

Early man and woman made their homes close to water. Not to enjoy the delights of an early morning dip but to have drinking water and to dispose of their waste matter. The first and only sanitary planning would have been when our ancestors realised that it was better to have the drinking place upstream from the one used as a 'convenience'.

European sanitary civilization started with the Minoans in Crete. They led the way in fittings, with a bath that closely resembled what we have today, flush latrines, drains and piped waters. All this in 2000 BC. No slouches either when it came to sanitation were the Egyptians, the Babylonians, the Jews and the Greeks who considered a quick cold bath to be rather a manly pastime. The Romans elevated bathing to an art form and would spend whole days rushing from hot water to tepid water to a cold plunge. So enjoyable was the Roman bathing experience that the Fall of the Roman Empire may have been due to excessive time in the bathroom and not enough attending to their provinces.

It will not have escaped you that all this cleanliness was taking place in warmer climes than North Yorkshire, an area not renowned for al fresco bathing. However, research has shown that we may not have

Our recent sanitary past. A brick built two-holer privy behind an old mill near Darlington. The washhouse in the background had two set pots, the largest for scalding a pig once a year, the other for the weekly wash. Every drop of water had to be carried to the washhouse.

been a sanitary wilderness. It is believed by some experts that heated stones were placed in natural pools in streams high up on the moors of the Northern Dales as far back as 2–3000 BC. Water could be brought up to boiling by this method and there is speculation that whilst cooking may have been the prime objective, a spot of communal bathing may also have taken place. A sort of Bronze Age party and barbecue.

The Romans were over here for nearly four hundred years but their funny ways never really caught on. They were very big on drains and hygiene, worshipping household gods that included Stercutius the god of manure and Cloacina the goddess of sewers. It was quite a relief when the Roman influence waned and we could revert to our old ways with no one to nag us to take a bath. Sadly the art of plumbing was lost in the Dark Ages with the subsequent invasions of Saxons, Danes and Jutes.

The early Church was a bit muddled about hygiene with very mixed views on bathing. Saints Agnes, Jerome and Catherine of Siena considered dirtiness to be a sign of holiness in which belief Saint Francis of Assisi also joined them. Pope Gregory thought bathing alright as long as it did not become 'a time wasting luxury'. Other holy men quite liked a bath but held back as an act of denial. Aldred the chronicler of Fountains and Kirkstall Abbeys in Yorkshire found it useful to sit in a bath of ice cold water up to his neck awaiting his 'worldly thoughts' to subside.

Later on there seems to have been some inkling that the odd bath, a bit of head shaving and foot washing was quite a good idea. The monks of Kirkstall, Fountains and Jervaulx Abbeys certainly knew the importance of running water. The Cistercians at Fountains Abbey, eight miles north of Harrogate, had privies set against a wall, divided by partitions and each with drainage below. Nine arches for nine latrines can still be seen. The reredorter or privy at the back of the monastic dormitory and the laver or conduit for the monks to wash their face and hands was superior to anything in the outside world.

We can still view the sophisticated sanitary arrangements of the Carthusian monks at Mount Grace Priory, founded in 1398, twelve miles north of Thirsk. Their way of life was less communal than other Orders and they had their own individual cells with a garden. Each cell had a latrine set over a stone channel flushed by running water from the springs on the hillside. The latrine had a wooden seat and often a niche for a candle. The stone channel foulwater drains were also flushed with running water. In addition each cell had water from a bronze tap set outside the garden door. The beautifully preserved remains, looked after by English Heritage, can be visited in their wooded tranquil setting off the A19.

Oh for the fragrance of the Carthusian arrangements: outside was rather beastly. Life in a castle was conducted with little privacy and few drains. Draughty garderobes or privies were set into the thickness of the castle wall with a wooden seat over the shaft that dropped down into a pit, moat, ditch or in some cases down the outside walls. Middleham Castle may have been an exception with access to a latrine tower that projected beyond the curtain wall. That much maligned King Richard III apparently preferred Middleham to his other castles and, who knows, the state of his garderobes may have been a factor.

Mount Grace Priory with the remains of the flush latrines built at the back of each cell. A visit to this lovely place will reveal just how advanced the Carthusians were in their sanitary arrangements. (By kind permission of English Heritage)

The view from Middleham Castle, once known as the 'Windsor of the North' and now in the care of English Heritage.

Garderobe construction was pretty basic and our ancestors saw no reason to improve on their original design. The Gold Hole Tower (did someone have a sense of humour?) of the early Norman castle at Richmond contained the garderobes. The lower part is 11th century with a spot of rebuilding work on the upper part in the 14th century containing a room with a fireplace and another garderobe. Three hundred years and no improvement.

A magnificent garderobe construction can be seen on a visit to Skipton Castle, stronghold of the Clifford family. The 'Long Drop' is situated off the mediaeval kitchen in an alcove jutting from the outside wall. Waste deposits went down the outside wall into the stream below and kitchen waste went down another chute next to it. Beneath the walls of Skipton Castle would not have been a place to linger.

***

For the better off baths were rare but not unknown. Made of wood, round and often padded inside to prevent an injudicious splinter, they could be lengthened to make room for others. It was considered a nice gesture to offer an honoured guest a bath and even more friendly for the host family to get in there with them. Food and drink were eaten while bathing, something the physicians of the day thought unwise, and if you were feeling very jolly you had your minstrels play music in the background. Water had to be heated and carried for all this to take place so only the wealthy with servants could have the experience.

However dear our friends are to us this is not something we would wish to consider now but different ideas of privacy prevailed in mediaeval Britain. Indeed in present times for those with a young family, often the bathroom is the only place to escape to for some peace and quiet and anyone who has ever tried a romantic bath for two knows that someone always gets the tap end and has to sit on the plug!

The only body parts that people were concerned with were their hands. It was customary when eating up at the castle to use hands for serving and eating. You either washed in the stone basin called the lavatoria, lavabos or lavers at the entrance to the dining hall or the person sitting next to you poured water from a jug over your hands held over a bowl. These washbasins and jugs were often costly and highly decorated. In 1444 a Northallerton gentleman left, in his will, four basins and two jugs for washing at table. Someone was maintaining standards in North Yorkshire.

A 15th century *Boke of Curtasye* offered helpful advice: 'Let thy fingers be clean. Thou must not put thy fingers into thine ears, or thy hands on the head' – lice being a problem. 'The man who is eating must not be cleaning by scraping with his finger at any foul part.' Which foul part we are not told. The book covers everything from not playing with cats and dogs at meal times, not spitting on the table and if you have to blow your nose, wipe your hand afterwards on your skirt or tippet. Etiquette demanded that you do not pick your teeth with a knife, nor clean them with the tablecloth and if you wash your mouth at table do not spit the water back into the basin but decently onto the floor. Finally an admonishment against something that has always been considered a bad social gaffe: 'Beware of thy hinder parts from gunblasting.'

Elizabeth I was considered highly eccentric because she took a bath once a month, 'whether she need it or no' – her courtiers never, relying instead on heavy perfumes to disguise the smell. Her Majesty rejected the garderobe for the more comfy close stool, an elaborate box with padded seat and lid into which a pewter chamber pot was placed, but she failed to see the possibilities of her godson Sir John Harington's flush water closet invention with new fangled valve.

It was during the reign of Elizabeth that disaster struck what was then the important market town of Wensley for in 1563 the Plague devasted the town. A few miles away at East Witton, villagers took the only precautions known to them. Andrea Robson lives in the oldest house in the village, dating from the 1200s, and round the inside of the front door the fearful inhabitants painted – sheep dip. Sheep represented wealth and what was good enough to keep a sheep healthy was certainly good enough for humans. Whatever was in the sheep dip, it worked as that household kept clear of the Plague and the house remained standing.

All this was taking place far from London and the people of North Yorkshire had no time to consider life at Court. Life may have been harsh but it was not any better in the capital. To escape the Plague in London in 1665, Charles II and his entourage went visiting. A doubtful honour for his hosts and with not enough close stools to go round courtiers relieved themselves behind curtains or in any convenient nook or cranny.

***

With the fork coming into general use in the 18th century we stopped washing even our hands. Life became grimmer and you ventured into town at your peril. Whilst there were some public latrines built over rivers, the preferred disposal was the 'pysse potte' out of the upstairs window. Water in towns was piped intermittently from any nearby river but as that was invariably highly polluted with waste matter, it did not do you a lot of good. The invention of a closet washed out with water into an efficient sewage system was the dream of many an inventor but the combination of dodgy valves, weak flushes and poor disposal meant that those early WCs often caused more problems than they solved.

At the start of the reign of Victoria in 1837 little progress had been

A typical village pump at Castle Bolton in Wensleydale.

achieved on the bathing or lavatory front since Roman times. Even Her Majesty was without a proper bathroom, making do with a commode and a portable bath in the bedroom. Buckingham Palace cannot have been too clean as the company Tiffin & Son was proud to boast of their services as 'bug destroyers to Her Majesty'. As if this were not enough, underneath Windsor Castle, Prince Albert found 53 overflowing cesspits. Victoria was enormously lucky in her choice of husband; if he had not been a prince he would have been a jolly fine plumber. With typical Germanic thoroughness he sorted out his wife's plumbing but died before finishing the job.

In fact Her Majesty did better when she travelled by train and it is not generally known that Victoria was a keen 'railway buff' and 'train spotter'. In the National Railway Museum in York her favourite carriage, used from 1869 to 1895, is displayed in all its opulent glory. Between the sitting room and bedroom is a small bathroom, complete with washbasin and substantial taps and a lavatory with pull-up handle at the side and fine wooden seat. The walls are upholstered in blue plush velvet and even the ceiling is done in white velvet and padded. After the death of her manservant and friend John Brown, an Indian, Abdul Karim, known as 'The Munshi', took over and he had his own bathroom, complete with lavatory, at the end of the carriage.

It seems fitting to end this chapter with the shortcomings of royal plumbing because it places in context what is to follow. From the highest in the land to the lowest we were united in our struggle to keep clean. Her Majesty in her bath in front of the fire was no better off than the humble Dalesman, except she had a servant to heat the water and she probably never shared her water with Albert. Country privies were a cut above town commodes and with fresh air and largely unpolluted rivers, country people enjoyed a healthier lifestyle. Yet even here there are dark tales to tell of less than pristine privies and folk who were strangers to the bathroom, so let us turn our attention to how people kept clean and decent in North Yorkshire.

Harsh Words

——— ⚬⚬ ———

'Those piggish nuisances are shortly to be removed; but I am not so sanguine as to believe it . . . although the salaried roadster was seen the other day with a scraper on his shoulder.' Letter to the Wensleydale Advertiser, 7th November 1848.

There is much to see and do in the little market town of Hawes nestling at the western end of Wensleydale. The Dales Countryside Museum, the Wensleydale Creamery famous for the cheese, the Ropemakers, interesting shops, cafes and pubs, all make for a delightful day out. Little does the casual visitor realise that a stroll round Hawes was not always so sweet and that the sanitary past was far from pleasing.

The Dales Countryside Museum kindly allowed me access to their Study Room to view some old copies of the *Wensleydale Advertiser* and before I proceed further I must heed a former Editor writing on 23rd April 1844. 'We have some FRIENDS who do us the honour of copying from our paper, but omit to make an acknowledgement: we shall thank them to be more candid in future or we must gibbet them.'

The *Wensleydale Advertiser* from 1841 to 1849 devoted considerable column inches to the disgraceful state of sanitation and hygiene in Hawes. 'Warning of Cholera – There is perhaps, no little town in the North of England, that so much needs those precautionary measures as Hawes.' (Note for future visitors – all is well now.) A lively correspondence ensued, pulling no punches.

A letter to the paper dated 23rd December 1844 from 'A Rate Payer' called the attention of the Surveyors of the High Roads 'to the nuisances which exist in this township, from the habit of throwing ashes on the side of the Roads, and also from depositing manure and coal heaps thereon'. A Yorkshireman tough on law and order, he went

Hawes circa 1910 when the cattle market was still held in the main street. How did the ladies in the centre of the picture keep their skirts clean? (Ann Holubecki Collection)

on to write that if nothing was done the Surveyors should be summoned before the Petty Sessions.

Officialdom, in the shape of Surveyors, moved pretty slowly. In spite of generally held discontent, it was not until nearly three years later on 31st August 1847 that the *Wensleydale Advertiser* reported the matter of the drains erupting again: 'A notice signed by a number of inhabitants had been served on the Surveyor requesting him to proceed forthwith in making the drain in the Holme in Hawes and in removing the present filthy nuisance there from the evacuation of the public drains, otherwise he would be proceeded against according to the highway regulations. After a desultory conversation in which some very inelegant and coarse remarks were made a resolution was made.' Ah, the cut and thrust of debate in public affairs!

Three months later – still no progress with the Surveyor. A Resident wrote, 'The street is now left and has been for a long time in such a state that no pedestrian can cross it without being nearly up to the knees . . . The fault must rest somewhere – we have hired a surveyor, and I suppose he is now in Lancashire or somewhere, trying to earn an honest crust.' Obviously a stubborn man and seeking sanctuary across the border.

A year later and another letter dated 7th November 1848: 'Last night, I unfortunately had the imprudence to attempt a passage through Kitty Chapman Street, and in order to avoid tumbling over churns, milk cans, budgers,' (a milk back pan used when milking out in the fields) 'and other remblements so frequently exposed there, I swerved a little too far south, and with my left foot went slap into a sumphole – lost my equilibrium and then came down on all fours.

'I have since been told, Mr Editor, that those filthy and (allow me to use the expression) those piggish nuisances are shortly to be removed; but I am not so sanguine as to believe it. It is my fixed opinion that they will remain with us the whole winter, although the salaried roadster was seen the other day with a scraper on his shoulder. I would therefore, earnestly recommend the introduction of "stilts" especially to those who wish to preserve untarnished, the brilliant jet of Braithwaite's blacking.

'I am, as people say, getting up in years; yet, I am determined to try

The beautiful old Bishopdale farmhouse of Avril and John McGregor, built in 1640 by George Fryer and his wife. The dark two-holer privy was last used forty years ago when a famous Yorkshire walking stick maker Tom Dinsdale lived here.

the experiment and shall order a pair from Jonny the first time I see him. In the hopes that the above may be of service to (at least) some of your readers.

I remain, Mr Editor
Yours &c.,
Old Frank'

The Editorial comment joined Old Frank and castigated people who 'look upon the sanitary agitation in Hawes as complete nonsense', giving dire warning that if the Cholera did not get them, the Typhus would.

It is a relief to note that the the first Public Health Act in the cholera year of 1848 made it law for a fixed sanitary arrangement to be fitted to every household. We must be ever thankful for this, otherwise the people of Hawes would either have been wiped out, or walking on stilts!

***

I do not want to paint a picture of unrelenting filth here in North Yorkshire, because it would not be true. Many communities were vigilant over the state of their roads and rivers and none more so than Bainbridge, a picturesque village with a handsome green halfway along Wensleydale. A stroll on the banks of the Bain will still reveal long disused privies backing onto the river. Local historians assure me that the villagers rarely availed themselves of the instant disposal afforded by the running water but preferred to waste nothing and plough their goodness back into the land.

They also relished the abundant free supply of crayfish and woe betide anyone who messed with their river. An extract from the Records of the Lords Trustees of the Manor of Bainbridge noted that in 1757 George Metcalfe, commonly called Butcher George, was fined ten shillings 'for watering hides or skins in the River Bain, also for hanging the same on the Bridge and Sides of the Road about Bainbridge to the publick Nusance of the said Roads.' He was fined again fourteen years later for 'Laying raw Hides In the River Bain & Spreading them on the Town Green.'

Amy Scarr of Bainbridge remembered the crayfish back in the 1920s. The river ran past the Yorebridge Grammar School and one day there was the most tremendous flood, so much so that the river rose and flooded the girls' privies, flushing the contents out into the river. Amy recalled how excited they were sitting up in the high school windows watching the torrent. The next day there was a funny smell in the school, which got worse as time went on. Eventually Mr Shorter the headmaster called a joiner in to take up the floorboards. Underneath they found hundreds of dead crayfish that had been washed there by the flood.

Matters were also arranged with some thought in Masham at the eastern end of the Dales. This small town with its fine market square, handsome houses and imposing church set a high standard. Susan Cunliffe-Lister in her book *Days of Yore – A History of Masham* writes of the stringent byelaws and fines passed by the Masham Manor Court for the townsfolk in the 18th century:

> No-one shall lay anything that is noysum in the streets nor wash them in the town's wells.
> No-one shall tether horses on the Sabbath or night time on town fields.
> Swine must be kept rung.
> Water courses must be kept scoured.
> Geese and swine must not be put on Town Pasture without taking gates.

You could be fined one shilling in Masham for throwing rubbish into the street, one shilling and sixpence for having broken fences and one shilling for running unrung pigs in the town streets (unrung pigs were those without a ring through their noses – putting a ring through the pig's nose stopped it digging in the ground and, thus, prevented it from making a mess). A very valiant effort at cleaning up.

***

All was comparative sweetness in the country compared with the major towns of North Yorkshire. In the 1850s the people of Harrogate considered their town to be a very healthy place. In fact they had

An early high level water closet, still with a powerful flush, behind Margaret McGill's Georgian house in Masham. Before this installation buckets of night soil and chamber pots were collected from the bottom of the garden by the local pigman.

The author by the trough that supplied water for the cattle and horses at Castle Bolton in Wensleydale. (Photograph Ann Holubecki).

nothing to be complacent about, for in dry weather fifteen inches of sewage lay in Coppice Beck. That this beck ran to Knaresborough and the people there took their drinking water from it . . . well it was not Harrogate's problem. An outbreak of scarlatina, when several children died, stirred the authorites into action, though perhaps action is too strong a word; it was a further ten years before anything was done.

York, the great tourist honeypot of North Yorkshire, was in years gone by a place you visited at your peril; especially in the summer months when you were more than likely to pick up some very nasty diseases as a souvenir of your stay. As far back as the 1300s, Edward III complained that of all his cities the smell of York was the most offensive. This was saying something as most English cities were perfectly disgusting. However, York was to become even more offensive over the next five centuries.

A report of 1831 by the Central Board of Health expressed in strong language the lack of drainage in York. 'By this great defect houses, dung-heaps, pig sties etc. which unfortunately subsist in the heart of the town, are represented as pouring their fetid contents into open drains and the effluvia to be sometime such as might alone suffice to generate contagion.'

From 1831 to 1844 some improvements were made to the drainage but the greatest stumbling block was the damming up of the Foss for the sake of navigation, seven feet above the level of the Ouse. Those living on the side of the Foss were subjected to 'the influences of stagnant water, replete with vegetable and animal matters'. Those living in the streets bordering the side of the Ouse were constantly flooded with this noxious water. Added to this was the fact that the burial grounds in York were of great antiquity and the wells tainted from the contents of the graveyards; it was not uncommon to see bones lying about! I think I have already written enough to give you the general picture of life in York; you would have been lucky to reach the age of forty. Time to head for the hills!

Private Moments

—— 🐦 ——

'An outdoor privy is the quickest way of curing morning sickness.'
Denny Minnitt of Askrigg.

We now turn our attention to private matters: the privies and baths of North Yorkshire – rich in humour and much else besides. I needed help in this delicate quest and where else to turn but to the readership of those great Northern newspapers: *The Northern Echo*, the *Darlington and Stockton Times* and the *Craven Herald*. The taps were turned full on as a result of my plea for sightings of tin baths and privies. Anyone who has ever bathed in front of the fire or used an outside privy never forgets the experience.

The positioning of a privy cannot be overstated. The distance from the house was finely calculated; far enough away to overcome any smell but not so far that the walk there became a problem. The prevailing wind together with ease of emptying had all to be considered. There are many villages like Askrigg in Wensleydale where the houses huddle together and passages or ginnels shared with neighbours could cause problems if neighbours 'fell out'. Elma Banks' father owned property in the village and on his deeds the lawyers made it very clear: 'Access to the privy at all times.'

Ann Coates of Sowerby wrote to me of her childhood privy at Kilburn Park Farm near Thirsk. 'A stone toilet stood in the middle of the garden with a lovely view of the flowerbeds. It had two large seats with a small one in the middle. Little lids with handles covered the holes and big square lids folded down. There was coco matting on the floor and always the *Farmers Weekly* to read and "use". In winter when the wind was in the east it was not wise to linger or one had a very cold bottom. In summer flies crawled where they shouldn't and it was a case of flick them off and look sharp. When the piles of ". . . ." were high

No longer used for washing, a set pot makes an attractive plant container at the entrance to the substantial three-holer privy of Mr and Mrs John Hurlstone.

under the seats they were poked down with a stick until the lot was reluctantly emptied. I associate the rotted residue with rhubarb as the emptied pile was covered with sods, left for one year and then put onto the rhubarb.'

Country people are always aware of the weather and the changing seasons. An outside privy gave you more opportunity than you might wish to study and experience North Yorkshire weather. A hot summer brought smells and flies, autumn gales created strong updraughts; but winter was the cruellest time of all. Thomas Kirkbride remembered, 'not with pleasure the earth closet at the bottom of the garden in Askrigg. It was avoided if possible on cold winter nights. In emergencies we had to walk through the snow and it was no joke, to sit there sometimes in freezing conditions.'

Mrs Yewdall in the market town of Skipton had similar memories. 'We had to cross our backyard for a visit to the toilet, which until the 1930s didn't have a flush – just a water tap and bucket. A visit on a

A quiet corner of Ruth Raw's lovely garden in Carperby in Wensleydale. The two-holer privy used ashes from the fire and was cleaned from the back into the farmyard.

bleak winter's night was deferred as long as possible. It required dressing as for a visit to the Arctic, accompanied by a guttering candle to give some heat and light, as one sat beside icicles hanging from the tap, reading the cut up newspaper squares hanging behind the door.'

As if the outdoor privy experience was not enough, if you lived on a farm there were other hazards. Ivy Dale of Ripon remembered her father's farm in the 1930s at Kirklington between Bedale and Ripon. 'The two-holer was a walk across the farmyard near the stables. My brother, who was five years younger, had to be taken and as you sat there with only the light of a stable lamp you could hear the horses stamping and making a noise. We were too frightened to come out and mother had to rescue us.'

Margaret Chalmers of Grassington had a very nasty experience in a privy in Swaledale in 1938. 'I was aged nine and on holiday with relatives. I had to go across the cobbled yard to the brick built privy

Mary and Tommy Alderson's two-holer privy high up in Newbiggin looking towards Addlebrough and last used in the 1940s. The garden path had gooseberry bushes on each side and you were careful of the prickles. A flashlight was put in the window and the Yorkshire Post *served as paper.*

which was all whitewashed inside. In the wall by the side of the seat was a shute and I thought that was where the paper was kept. I plunged my hand down for some paper and felt something wet and horrible. It was a pig's snout! I rushed screaming out into the yard with my knickers round my ankles. The privy was right by the pigsty and the slops went down that shute. The paper, of course, was hanging in squares on the back of the door.'

Spiders and flies were always a hazard but angora rabbits? Eleanor Dinsdale of Carperby in Wensleydale recalled an incident at Appersett. 'I was about eight years old and we were visiting an aunt and uncle who kept angora rabbits. When they cleaned the cage out they would put the rabbit into the privy for safe keeping. I remember climbing the two steps up to the privy, throwing back the lid and sitting down. It was dark in there, then my eye caught a sudden movement at the back of the door, I jumped up again, without waiting to see what it was, and as quick as a flash I was out of that door. Of course if I hadn't been so quick, I would have seen it was a rabbit and I wouldn't have been frightened. As it was, I fled and the rabbit escaped down the privy hole. There was hell to pay, as not only had the rabbit escaped, but when it was caught, it had to be washed – for obvious reasons.'

The privy must have been daunting to a small child and Alice Leneghan of Sutton-in-Craven explained how children managed. 'When the little ones were being weaned from the potty to the privy it was one of the older ones' job to take him or her to the privy and give support, so that the little bottom did not go too far down the hole. Poor little souls were very frightened until they got used to it. In winter this was not a popular job and we were given dire threats to make us do the job properly.'

You could not count on any privacy, despite the fact that 'privy' is from the Latin 'privatus' meaning apart or secret. Indeed many people enjoyed the companionship of someone at the next hole or in the privy adjoining. Kathleen Wheater of Dacre Banks Women's Institute in Nidderdale knew of two old ladies who had been neighbours for 40 years. Their privies were at the bottom of the garden and they had always been in the habit of going down the garden at the same time every morning, sitting on their adjacent privies and having a chat through the wall. The landlord put a toilet inside their homes in 1964 but one old lady complained, 'It's no'un the same, Mary love, it's not as friendly as it was. I don't see thee every day now.'

Sometimes there could be an unwelcome intrusion such as encountered by Stella Kelly of the Burton Leonard Yorkshire Countrywomen's Association. 'We had a brick built privy with a shoulder high partition dividing it from the coalhouse. The tin bath was also kept in there hung on the door. One day I was sitting there when the coalman delivered a load of coal – he did beat a hasty retreat.'

A gentleman from Newsham near Richmond vividly recalled as a ten year old sitting on a two-holer on his friend's farm. He and the farmer's son liked nothing more than to go rat catching and helping generally. On this occasion he was bagging the husks after the corn had been threshed when he needed the privy. One of the women working on the threshing machine came and joined him there and with great aplomb, whilst adjusting her apparel said, 'Don't worry honey, sit still and carry on.' He went as red as a beetroot and sat still, rooted to the seat with embarrassment.

A woman who could always count on being alone in a privy was the pipe smoking great grandmother of Margaret Ryder of Knaresborough. 'She was a great character and would go off and tramp round the farms in the area looking for work. She said she could do the same work as a man, indeed the top of her thumb had been chopped off in an accident with a turnip cutter. She was also good at women's work too and would do washing for people. Mind, you had to be careful, because if she saw a petticoat she fancied; it disappeared! She would visit her granddaughter, my mother, who lived alone in the village of Low Laithe near Pateley Bridge. This remarkable old lady also smoked a pipe. When my father came courting my mother, he did not like great grandmother smoking in the house, so she would withdraw to the privy. Clouds of smoke could be seen coming from the privy and no one else could use it for ages after.'

A well loved privy was that belonging to Dorothy and Keith Smith of Low Spelderbanks Farm near Masham. Keith was brought up on the farm and the privy was fifty yards from the back of the house. Just outside the privy door was a magnificent dark red peony planted by his granddad who was a gardener at Sutton Grange. It was his pride and joy and he kept a proprietorial eye on it. When Keith as a boy had to

The privy at Low Spelderbanks Farm near Masham. A relative who left here for the bright lights of Pudsey declared you needed a number ten bus to get from house to privy. Cattle were the other side of the partition wall.

Keith Smith, with daughter Janet, still has the stable lamp that lit the privy at Low Spelderbanks Farm. If it was windy you were fighting to keep it going.

keep the privy path swept and weeded he would be there telling him to 'Mind that peony'. Later Keith's mother took over the care and guarded it religiously. When she finally moved away the peony went with her. It was a kind of family heirloom.

Sometimes a privy was in such a state that it was more than flesh and blood could stand. A lady of Bishopdale told me the story of when she moved into her cottage in the 1950s. The bathroom consisted of an iron bath with hot water cylinder and an outside privy which was full. She refused to use that privy, even when it had been cleaned out and installed instead a freestanding, chemical Elsan in the house. However, even this was too much for her granddaughter when she came to stay. She insisted on being driven to the public lavatories at Buckden in Wharfedale, a round trip of eleven miles!

The coming of the Elsan was a temporary relief although many regarded its installation as succumbing to fancy ways. Margaret Hadaway wrote from Gargrave near Skipton, to tell me of life with her two sisters Edith Quick and Nancy Edmondson as 'railway children', living on the side of the Settle to Carlisle railway. Their father John Stainton Dawson, known as Jack, was a plate layer and looked after the Blea Moor tunnel with three others. They moved to Blea Moor in 1939 to a railway cottage with no road, no electricity, just candles and oil lamps, and no water in the house, only a tap and stone sink in the outside washhouse.

On the end of the washhouse was the privy, a draughty single-seater over a deep hole, which they could only remember being cleared once. Edith tried once to pour the soapy water from washday down the privy but it only made matters worse by 'stirring things up' and mother was cross. Later on the London, Midland and Scottish Railway Company supplied the family with a chemical toilet. It was very small and unlike the earth privy had to be emptied frequently. Father steadfastly refused to use it and furthermore was adamant that, 'Them us use it mun empty it!' He maintained that the fell and a dockleaf was all that was needed. A man of principles of whom we will hear more.

People managed well enough at home but on public occasions life could be difficult. Josephine Hopper of Thoralby recalled for me the Bainbridge Sports Day held every June in a local field. She remembered as a child in the 1950s the delights of the trotting horse races, the motor cycle hill climb, the fancy dress and the misery of the

The coming of the Elsan to this house in Bishopdale was not greeted with enthusiasm by everyone.

This four-holer was used until the early 1950s by the residents of what was known as the Almshouse or Hospital of St John Baptist in Kirkby Ravensworth, founded in 1556 by John Dakyn LLD. It was built over a fearsome drop of some ten feet and used by both sexes but the end hole has been adapted for gentlemen.

lengthy queues formed for the only lavatory available for ladies. After complaints, the all male Sports Committee tried to rectify the situation and designed a loo they assumed would reduce the waiting time. It was a kind of a hen house with a four-holer and buckets inside. Unfortunately there were several things wrong with the design concept. Firstly the four holes were set so far back that no one could sit on them without their feet leaving the ground, secondly the idea of several Dales ladies going in at the same time was not one that the ladies were prepared to consider. Next year the queues remained as long as ever and the male committee wondered why.

Public amenities were often found 'wanting' as Olga Leathley of Masham Women's Institute illustrated with the tale of her husband's visit to a pub privy at Fearby Cross in the 1950s. After using the outside privy he complained to the pub landlord about the number of flies in there. To which the landlord replied, 'You should 'ave gone up

The school is now a house but the old school privy at Horsehouse still stands. The boys' side is seen clearly and the present owner Anne Readshaw with son Thomas stand in front of the section into which the contents were scraped prior to disposal by 'Uncle'.

there at dinner time then t' flies would have been down here in t' pub!'

Margaret Ryder visited a pub at Langdale End many years ago with her husband. There was no sign of a 'gents' and so her husband asked the elderly landlady for directions. 'Outside in t' barn,' she replied. As he was going outside she shouted after him, 'Watch out for t' hoss – it bites!' He was quick about it.

Schools certainly had to manage matters better. Horsehouse in Coverdale had a well built set of privies for about thirty pupils behind the small school. Boys were one side, girls the other. Each side had a wooden seat with a hole over a pit. The pit contents were cleared into a central section running between the two sets of privies and then covered with ashes from the school fire. Joyce Walker and Dorothy Suttill of Coverdale were at school in Horsehouse in the late 1920s and early 1930s and never remember a smell. They have fond memories of a local farmer known as 'Uncle' who would come and clear the central section out. Miss Waddington the teacher and her maid had a separate privy with a high wall in front of the door.

This reminded me of a story I heard at Wensleydale Probus of a village schoolteacher withdrawing to her teacher's privy for a few reflective moments, when suddenly a child's face appeared underneath the gap at the bottom of the door and a little anxious voice said, 'Please miss, should I give out t' pencils now?'

Robert Harker of Melmerby in Coverdale remembered when he and his brother Alan were at West Witton school in the early 1940s. The teacher had a separate privy with an opening at the back and they delighted in pushing stinging nettles up the back hole onto an unsuspecting bottom. The teacher would emerge rubbing the offending part and they all got caned for it.

Variations on this theme are always told by men who are now pillars of the community. Cecil Moore of Carperby in Wensleydale recalled quietly removing the flagstone that covered the small aperture at the back of the girls' privy at Downholme school in the 1940s and shoving stinging nettles up the hole. The boys for idle amusement used to see who could pee the highest. Happy days!

Mischief Night on 4th of November was a night to be careful. The night before the 'Plot' when the Yorkshireman Guy Fawkes attempted to blow up the Parliament of James I was marked by children playing tricks on unsuspecting adults. These could be tapping at windows, ringing doorbells and running away, daubing door handles with treacle and removing gates. The privy was not a good place to linger on 4th of November. Little boys would open the door and throw a penny banger in, or if there were two privies side by side, tie together the two 'snecks' or door latches, leaving the occupants imprisoned.

The opportunity for a joke was never far away with a privy. Andrea Robson's grandparents lived at Agglethorpe Hall in Coverdale. When she and her husband Keith were courting he was taken to Agglethorpe Hall to meet the grandparents. Andrea did not let on that her grandparents had all mod cons upstairs in the Hall but instead directed him to the outside two-holer privy. He came back much later saying he had used it but he did not know whether he should have put a leg down each hole!

Taking the Plunge

—— ❧ ——

'There are classes of labourers and mechanics, whose health would be preserved and their lives prolonged, if they knew how much depended on periodical cleansing.' Wensleydale Advertiser 1844.

After all this rather earthy talk, time to freshen up a little. Let us soak for a while in the warm waters of the tin bath in front of the kitchen fire and marvel at just how difficult it was to keep clean and decent. A bathroom was not considered to be a necessity for the lower orders and even that champion of cleanliness Prince Albert, in his design of the ideal working class cottage for the Great Exhibition of 1851, included a water closet but no bathroom.

It was difficult to keep clean when every drop of water had to be carried from a well, an outside tap or collected in a rainwater trough outside the back door. Once in the house it had to be heated in a side boiler of the kitchen range or in the set pot normally used for clothes, then transferred to either a bath or a basin and finally carried from the house to be emptied.

Cleanliness and Godliness were inexplicably linked in the Victorian mind. A certain Reverend Gentleman was reported in the pages of the *Wensleydale Advertiser* on 20th January 1846 as casting aspersions on the Wesleyans of Gayle. 'They came into the place clonking in those abominable clogs, and with such dreadful dirty faces that I was disgusted with their appearances, and above all their conduct in eating was most enormous beyond my language to describe: some had actually come without any dinner to satiate themselves for the small charge of sixpence each.'

Quite rightly the Editor was not going to let this pass and thought that 'If ye cannot say weel – say nowt!' He even suggested with a flash of Yorkshire sarcasm that the Revd Gentleman might prefer the

Water was collected from the roof into a large stone tank with a tap at one end. This one is at Burn House, Askrigg. (Photograph Ann Holubecki)

Wesleyans to come barefoot so as to give him less offence.

However, the Revd Gentleman had his comeuppance on 17th February with a strongly worded reply from one who was there. 'This individual came to a tea festival held in the Wesleyan Chapel at Gayle; uninvited – that he partook of such hospitality, making no renumeration, even to the extent of a double share; on a succeeding night we find him at the festival at West Witton using those words in reference to the kindness with which he was received where his company was unsolicited.'

We must not make too harsh a judgement on people like Tom 'Tipster', the man who emptied the night soil in Glasshouses in Nidderdale in the 1900s. Audrey Holmes of Bilton Women's Institute recounted a family story of the day Tom 'Tipster' stopped his cart, leaned on it and said plaintively to her husband's grandfather, 'My feet are killing me!' Grandfather said, 'Have you tried washing them?' Next time he saw him, Tom 'Tipster' was delighted to report that he had taken the advice and his feet were a lot better.

Geraldine Coates of Grinton in Swaledale told me of another gentleman who was a stranger to his bathtub who lived in Swaledale in the 1950s. He had to go to his doctor about one of his feet which was troubling him and only washed the one the doctor was going to look at.

However, many people have fond memories of the tin bath and bath night. Doreen Yewdall wrote in her charming *Childhood Recollections* of the 1920s, 'We had very little money to spare for luxuries but my sister and I had a full and happy childhood. We lived down one of the many yards leading off the High Street in Skipton, in a stone built terrace house, comprising living kitchen, front room, three bedrooms and a cellar pantry – but no bathroom. Friday night was the family bath night. Down from its hook in the back yard, came the zinc bath. The fire was built up in the kitchen range to heat the water in the side boiler and with a blanket draped round the clothes horse, we were ready. My sister and I, one at each end of the bath, with Mum standing by with a lading can to top up the water, then, warm and dry, we were sent to bed with a cup of cocoa and a book to read while the bath was given over to Mum and Dad.'

Brenda Baldwin recalled a childhood high on the moors at Fryup in the 1940s. Her family had their own patch of peat that was dug up, left to dry and then used to make an excellent fire to heat the water in the boiler. 'You had to bring the water in a bucket from outside. The three children and Mum and Dad bathed in the tin bath in front of the fire. The water came from the moor and ran into an outside trough which was scrubbed out every Friday. We had to pull out a plug, scrub it out and then wait for it to fill up again. We had it for drinking as well and it was always fresh and cold.'

Sometimes the water was not always as crystal clear as one would wish. Jean Day of Thornton Rust spent holidays with her grandmother in her 1844 cottage in Wykeham near Scarborough. 'In the summer of 1946 I stayed six weeks and bathed once a fortnight in the tin bath in front of the kitchen range. All water was drawn from a tap across the backyard. As it was extremely hard water, Granny collected rainwater in a ribbed wash-tub by the back door to be used for morning ablutions in a bowl on the kitchen table and when washing her hair. I recoiled from using the rainwater as beetles and other creepy-crawlies fell into the tub washed down the pipe by the rain.'

Millie taking centre stage for this photograph of the tin bath found in the Aldersons'
barn at Newbiggin.

A keen gardener can make anything beautiful. Ruth Raw's tin bath in her garden at Carperby in Wensleydale.

Friday night seems to have been the most popular night for a bath although some favoured Saturday lunchtime ready for church the next day. Gwen Welton of Northallerton lived in the small village of Ellerbeck. 'Friday night was bath night and out came the wash tub by the fire and filled with water from the boiler. The fire range in the living room was blackleaded with a fairly large oven and side boiler along with a large kettle. One day when I was around fifteen years old I must have been in a dream as I put a shovel of coal in the side water boiler instead of on the fire! My did I really cop it for doing such a daft thing. We had a large fender round the fire which was quite wide and on baking day bread and teacakes were put on this to rise. When I was about five years old I decided to flatten all the teacakes when no one was around! Yes, I cop't it again!'

With all this effort there was no time to be fussy about sharing water. Mrs Garbutt of Bedale told me of the pecking order for baths in her childhood home in Great Smeaton in the 1930s: her first, then mother, the youngest son, two young uncles, granddad and finally dad.

Sophie Johnston, Jack Brittain and James Peacock enjoying a summer's afternoon in Castle Bolton. The tin bath, hand made by the local tinsmith Frank Shields, was in use up to the 1970s.

Father did not always partake because he could wash in the stable yard in the bothy up at Great Smeaton Hall. Mother put a couple of fresh scoops of hot water between bathers and Mrs Garbutt remembered it as lovely and steamy in front of the fire.

Diane Bell of Thoralby Women's Institute remembered her mother telling her that as the only girl she always went first, followed by her brother and then the boy from next door! John King of Romanby often popped round to his friends on a Friday night if they were in the bath. This was in the mid 1940s and in the summer the fire would be lit in the outhouse under the copper and the heated water from this went into a wooden barrel cut in two. He and his friend would be about twelve and the youngest about eight and they would all bath together. An enduring bond was forged as they are still all friends. However, there is a twist to this story for John had already had a bath two hours before at home, in front of the fire in winter, in the outside washhouse in summer. This probably made him the cleanest boy in all Yorkshire.

It was not that unusual to travel to your bath. Heather Peacock of Castle Bolton spent her childhood on a farm in Swaledale where her parents were tenants of the famous British aviator, Sir Thomas Sopwith. Whilst Sir Thomas might have been a dab hand with aeroplanes, his tenants were without a bathroom. They used to go to the farm opposite for a proper bath although they did have a rather posh hip bath painted a fetching shade of green by mother. Heather bathed in front of the fire in the living room, taking the water from a tap in the side boiler of the Yorkist range. Heather went first, then her sister, followed by a brother. Lux flakes gave you soapy water but the worst thing was having to empty it afterwards over the 'flags'. A bathroom and electricity were not installed until 1964, by which time Heather had left home in search of more sophisticated plumbing.

Mrs Carr of Settle spent her childhood living with granny at Winterburn, a side valley of Malhamdale. 'There was no water in the house and it had to be carried from the well, a distance of about one hundred yards. The water was heated on the side of the range and I can remember it took four buckets. I bathed in front of the fire every week, some of the family only every other week. My mother's brothers always disappeared before the bath because the last one in had to ladle the water out.'

Hard working farmers had no use for fancy toiletries. Toothpaste was a mixture of salt and soot in a jam jar, used on a brush and rinsed out. Soap was plain carbolic. Indeed Mrs Carr's aunt only ever used carbolic soap and had a beautiful complexion in old age, 'like a cherry'. Grandmother used carbolic soap on her hair as well, softening it with hot water to make a shampoo and then finishing off with coconut oil. 'When she died at eighty four she didn't have a grey hair.'

Yorkshire girls brought up on a farm were not encouraged to indulge in airs and graces, but some younger ones had their hair tied up in rags on a Saturday night, to produce a mass of ringlets and curls for church on Sunday. For others the memory of mother anxiously raking through their hair looking for nits with the 'biddy comb' will always be linked with bath night.

Another beauty tip came from Mary Bostock of Castle Bolton. Her great grandmother always washed her face in the morning with cold water from the outside water tank, often having to break the ice. She had a beautiful skin right up to her death in her late eighties. Those of

A bath with memories for Barry Tinkler. The farmhouse in Great Stainton had a bathroom but it was too cold in winter and the children were bathed on a Sunday night, two at a time in front of the kitchen fire, ready for school on Monday.

us who spend pounds on face creams to hold back the ageing process might like to consider the beneficial effects of hard work and cold water.

Mary's family home was fairly typical in that an outside WC was installed in 1937 but the bathroom had to wait until 1970. As a child Mary had her bath in front of the kitchen range but later she valued her privacy and would light a fire in the sitting room and carry her bath in there.

Margaret Wigham of Burton Leonard Yorkshire Countrywomen's Association was very impressed with friends who lived high on Dallowgill Moor. They used to boast that they had a marvellous bathroom, it even had colour television. Margaret thought this very posh, until she paid them a visit one day and saw the tin bath outside and realised they bathed in the kitchen. The colour television will give you a clue that this was not very far back – in the 1980s.

The 'railway family' of Blea Moor had tales to tell of bath night.

Margaret and Edith both remember bathing their young sister Nancy on the table in the big white enamel bowl, the same bowl in which the bread was made. When they were older they would take this bowl upstairs to have a good wash. 'Mother used to say, "You must wash down as far as possible, up as far as possible – and possible takes care of itself!" Occasionally we had a bath in front of the fire but often the bath was out of commission because the pig had been killed and was lying in it covered in saltpetre to preserve it. Once the joints were cut up and hung above the fire then we could have a bath.'

Life on Blea Moor was hard but the three girls were all healthy. As far as they can remember father never had a bath at Blea Moor but always a good top wash after working in the tunnel. He was of the school of thought that believed 'bathing weakens'. He rarely went out and when he did it was always signalled by a good wash and his trilby hat being placed on the piano, prior to leaving. One night Edith, who was newly married, was visiting with her husband Norman. 'Mother came into the room in a tizzy saying, "The Hat's on the piano!" Father walks in and says to Norman, "Is t' for a pint?" So off they go to walk the mile down the railway line to the pub near the Ribblehead Station, leaving mother very anxious. Father had quarrelled with the landlord and not set foot in the place for about five years. On his return Norman told us of the meeting. Joe the landlord looked up as Jack came in and said, "Now then Jack." Jack looked across, "Now then Joe." Long pause, then "Usual Jack?" "Aye, usual Joe." Norman was very impressed with the considered way the quarrel, whatever it had been about, was resolved.'

When Jack Dawson finally retired from the railway in 1956 he and his wife Lucy went to live at Winshaw off the Ribblehead to Hawes road. This house had the luxury of a bathroom and calor gas cooking. 'As far as anyone knows father used the bath only once. Soon after moving in mother ran him a bath and persuaded him to get in. Shortly afterwards he emerged from the bathroom and declared roundly that "If that's bathing I don't think I'll bother." We don't think he had a bath again but he was always very sweet smelling and looked pink and clean.'

***

It was a problem for everyone who bathed in the kitchen that they could always be interrupted by someone calling.

In the village of Gayle in Wensleydale the Insurance man always called on a Friday night for the premium; when the man of the house was in from work and before he had chance to get down to the pub and spend it. Friday night was bath night and the Insurance man always stayed chatting too long while the children had to remain in the tin bath behind the clothes horse, the water slowly getting colder.

Visitors were not welcome on bath night as shown in the tale told by Thomas Kirkbride. 'Our family lived in Askrigg up Silver Street or Pudding Lane it was sometimes called. We were born in the Great War years, my sister Margaret and brother Sid; Shelagh came much later. Sid and I had been bathed one Friday night near Christmas time and when it was Margaret's turn we were ordered from the kitchen to the parlour to sit with Father. Suddenly we heard a scream from Mother and dashed through to the kitchen. There were four lads stood there, their faces smeared with black and they had just walked in without knocking. This was a local custom near Christmas and they had a little verse, "Here comes I, nivver been afore, walked right in, wi'out knocking on the door!" They were lads who lived down the lane and their timing could not have been worse. Father grabbed his stick from the corner and chased them out!'

Mind you sometimes it was the visitor who received the shock. Harold Hammond, a renowned butcher in the Northern Dales, was delivering meat to a farmer's wife in Countersett high above Semerwater. He knocked on the door, 'Come in' she shouted and on entering there she was starkers in the tin bath in front of the fire! Many blushes all round for she was expecting her husband as it was around milking time but Harold, ever the gentleman, beat a hasty retreat.

Monday Morning Blues

—— ✑ ——

'Ez badly used ez a peggy-tub boddum.' A Yorkshire saying.

It would be hard to find a more soul destroying household chore than the unremitting drudgery of the weekly wash. For those who can remember their mothers tied to the mangle in the washhouse on a Monday there is profound admiration for what she managed to achieve with only hot water, soap and a huge amount of 'elbow grease'.

From time to time at the Dales Countryside Museum in Hawes there are demonstrations in the reconstructed Dales kitchen of the Victorian washday. It was here that I first met Ann Holubecki as she explained the uses for a number of very queer looking objects. An interested crowd gathered round with murmers of, 'I remember those, my Mum had one just like it.' Children stared in disbelief as she introduced us to some of the 'aids' to washday.

Much of the washday and kitchen paraphernalia had been collected by Ann's mother, who came into Wensleydale to make cheese in the early 1920s. She married Redvers Hopper, a local farmer and auctioneer, and when people were throwing out their old kitchen stuff, Margaret would be there to buy it. What a good job she had the foresight to amass this collection, otherwise most would have found its way onto the scrapheap or bonfire and a valuable insight into everyday life would have been lost.

For readers over a certain age, the words slopstone, posser, dolly tub, set pot and mangle will conjure up images of childhood. For others a short explanation might come in handy. A 'slopstone' was a shallow stone sink on which you scrubbed clothes or stood buckets. A 'posser' was a long wooden handle on the end of which was a circular, concave copper head and 'to poss' meant you vigorously moved this thing up and down, squeezing your washing in the wash tub. A 'dolly' was

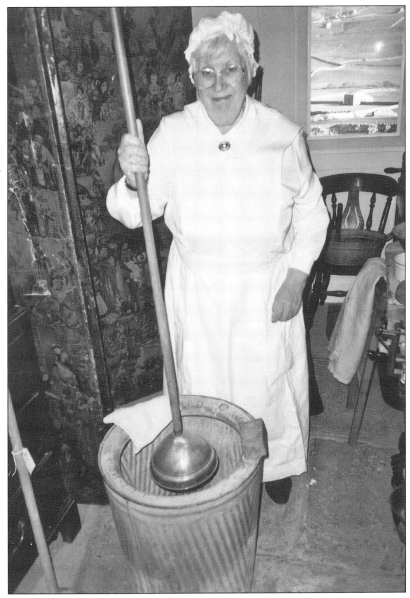

Ann Holubecki in the reconstructed Dales kitchen in the Dales Countryside Museum at Hawes with posser and ribbed dolly tub. (By kind permission of the Dales Countryside Museum)

Ann Holubecki demonstrating the Ewebank 'Rapid' Washer (circa 1910) used in Askrigg until the 1960s for washing blankets. (By kind permission of the Dales Countryside Museum)

another wooden instrument with a sort of four legged stool on the end used for agitating your washing by hand in the 'dolly tub' – a wash tub.

The 'set pot' or 'copper' was a large copper or cast iron bowl set into brickwork under which a fire was lit to heat the water in the bowl. The set pot was often in an outhouse and the water had to be carried to it. The bowl also came in handy for mixing and boiling the pigswill; a concoction of leftovers, potatoes and turnips. When the pig was fat enough to be killed the boiling water from the set pot was poured over the skin and the bristles could be scraped off the pig. Vegetarians will be reaching for a tissue by now. A 'piggin' or 'lading can' was used to fill and empty the set pot.

Lastly the 'mangle' to wring the clothes by passing them through wooden rollers turned by a large cast iron handle. This job was often allocated to children when they were strong enough to turn the handle. It was boring work and hands were best kept on the handle. A childhood friend still bears the marks of a flattened thumb caught between the rollers!

An early dolly peg used for agitating the washing, belonging to Raymond Jones of Great Burdon.

A typical slopstone in Mary Bostock's washhouse at Castle Bolton. (Photograph Ann Holubecki)

Mangles were considered quite a luxury item in early Victorian times. Ann told of a farmer's wife in Low Row in Swaledale who owned the only mangle in the village. She was an enterprising woman and charged one penny to the other women in the village to mangle a basket of washing.

There was little humour to be found in the washhouse, just hard work, backache and chapped hands. Alice Leneghan of Sutton-in-Craven belonged to a large family of five girls and two boys with 'a lovely caring mother' and she wrote to me of family life. 'Washday – when I press the button on my automatic washing machine, I think of mother. She got up early to light the copper fire in which to boil the "whites", there was the peggy tub (a large barrel-shaped wash tub), peggy legs and the big old mangle, with wooden rollers and a big wheel turned by hand (horse work!).

'How she coped washing for nine I don't know, as we got older someone helped her turn the mangle. Ironing was done by two flat irons in front of the fire. Mother baked all our bread and cakes. The

A cast iron set pot with a glazed brick surround in a washhouse on a farm just outside Askrigg.

flour was put in a large earthenware bowl called a "pancheon" and she kneaded it with the bowl on the hearthrug. It was someone's job to stand by with a jug of warm water to add a little at a time when told. She used to say, "Not too much, don't drown the Miller." I used to retreat to the privy as an excuse to escape the washing up or any other job I did not want to do!'

Doreen Yewdall in her *Childhood Recollections* wrote, 'Washing day was a marathon back in the 1920s and 1930s, no automatic washing machine then. When we arrived home from school on a Monday dinner time, the kitchen floor covering (coco matting) had been lifted and we had to sit and eat our dinner on a damp stone-flagged floor along with the dolly tub, possing stick and wringing machine all drying out after the morning's wash. Woe betide you if it was a wet day as wet washing would be hanging limply above you from cords strung across the kitchen. By teatime though, all would be back to normal, apart from the wet washing, of course.'

You needed an early start, so often you soaped your whites and your working clothes and left them soaking separately overnight in cold water. You would also fill the copper on Sunday ready for the 'off' on Monday. Very religious families who did not believe in work on a Sunday had to do the preparations on a Monday and so Tuesday was washday.

The water came from the stream or was collected from the roof into a large tank outside the backdoor. Mary Bostock of Castle Bolton had to climb into her tank and scrub it out, once a year in the summer when the water was low. Rainwater was considered best for washing as it was softer, therefore you used less soap. All of it had to be carried and if there were any 'wiggly things' in the water it had to be strained through a sile pad, normally used to strain the milk. You were very blessed if you had a cold water tap.

Gwen Welton of Northallerton remembered the sequence of events in her house. 'First we lit the fire under the copper boiler and then we possed the clothes in the dolly tub. The posser sucked the water through the clothes and hopefully the dirt as well. They were rinsed and put through the old mangle, then boiled in the copper boiler, rinsed again, through the mangle again and finally hung out in the orchard.'

Many farmers and workmen in North Yorkshire wore a 'kitle', a

The set pot and slopstone sink in a washhouse in Carperby. Water had to be carried to it across the yard when the present owner moved there in 1946. By 1947 a Versco washing machine with electric rollers had been installed in the house.

khaki brown overall coat for work. The kitle and other very dirty clothes had to be scrubbed, by rubbing on hard soap and using a scrubbing brush on the slopstone, before you could even begin to think about soaking them. In early days corrugated washboards (the sort I associate with Skiffle in the 1960s) made of wood, brass, copper, zinc or even glass were used to rub the washing on. Later dolly tubs had corrugated sides, so the washboards were redundant for all but the most stubborn stain.

Tackling stains was a tough job. Hard soap, made from rendered fat from sheep's wool and carcasses, was shredded or grated into hot water to make soap suds, or rubbed into the dirty cuffs and collars on a rubbing board or slopstone and soaked overnight in cold water with a handful of soda. Oxydol was one of the earliest washing powders and ammonia was a good rinsing agent for blankets. In the early days an easy supply of ammonia could be had from the chamber pot!

Washday was not helped by the fact that so much of everyday life was coloured white: bed linen, tablecloths, underclothes, petticoats and baby clothes. Children wore white aprons or pinafores to school, women wore long white aprons for most of the day – all had to be boiled. 'Dolly blue' was used in the rinsing water to keep everything sparkling white.

I was not a pretty child and it did not help that I was often to be seen with blue marks on my face, arms or legs as my mother was a great believer in appying the dolly blue bag to relieve stings and nettle rash!

Collars, cuffs, shirt fronts, pillow cases and especially aprons were all rinsed in Robins Starch at the end of the wash. According to Ann, the dirt came out better when an item had been starched. Clothes had to be tough to stand up to all this harsh treatment. Buttons were brass covered with linen, anything else would break in the mangle.

You can imagine the state of a woman's hands by the end of washday

This advertisement of 1898 emphasised the importance of the state of your washing. You would not want to let your husband down in front of his friends!

and it was not uncommon for the hands to be bleeding, especially if you were pegging out in a raw east wind. 'Whites' were put outside in frosty weather to help bleach them or when the sun shone they would be laid flat on a hedge or on clean grass.

It has been known to rain a bit in North Yorkshire and the farmers' wives often hung the washing out in the alleyway between the 'shippon' or cowshed and the farmhouse. The clothes dried well in the draught out of the rain and washing can still be seen hung out like this in some villages.

Imagine your feelings if after all this hard work someone made free with the washing while it was outside. The *Wensleydale Advertiser* reported on such an incident and used it to make a complaint about not enough police officers on the beat. All this in April 1844 – some things never change! 'On Tuesday night last two shirts were stolen from the garden of John Coulton, Esq., of Willow House Burtersett, where they were laid out to bleach, another from Richard Pratt of Burtersett, and a quantity of white yarn from Isabella Blake of the same place. We cannot but remark on the entire inefficiency as a detective force of the new Constablery [sic]; there were prints of a female foot (right and left shoes) at the place from whence Pratt's shirt was stolen, and from that and other circumstances we think that an active officer would easily have detected the depredators.'

Of course even when it was dry the end was nowhere in sight: everything had to be ironed. When I think of my lackadaisical laundering – it is a rare towel or undergarment that sees the bottom of a hot iron in this house – my female forebears would be horrified. Ironing took place on a blanket on the kitchen table. Solid flat irons called 'sad' irons were made in many different weights and sizes and they were used in pairs, one iron being used while the other heated on a trivet in front of the fire. You could test when the iron was hot enough by spitting on it.

Irene Stacey, a local writer from Richmond, recalled vividly that 'the flat irons were heated on the top rail of the fire and then placed in metal "slippers". It was touch and go sometimes whether a sooty mark befell a piece of ironing, be it a white tablecloth or a summer dress. It was a nightmare. I have always hated ironing!'

I give thanks for my steam iron with its multiple settings, as back then you had many irons to choose, from depending on the garment. A

Stephen Moffitt aged four who looks as if he might be up to mischief with that ball! Behind him in the passage alongside the village shop in Askrigg his grandmother Brenda Bowe hangs her washing. Stephen is the sixth generation to be associated with Sykes House in Askrigg.

An old box iron with slug belonging to Barry Tinkler of Bishopton. The nasty looking instrument is a turnip snagger. The benefits of turnips to Yorkshire wellbeing in the past is now often overlooked.

box iron with its heated slug inside would keep the ironing cleaner. Gardeners might think this is a suitable fate for these garden pests, but no, the slug was a piece of metal heated in the fire and placed in the box iron.

The types of irons were endless: there was a smaller box iron for baby clothes and cuffs, a smooth convex-bottomed 'glossing' iron to 'shine up' starched linen and cotton and a 'goffering' poker shaped iron for ruffles and frills. The opportunity to scorch your clothes was endless too.

Finally with relief you could place the now pristine, ironed washing on the clothes-horse, otherwise known as the winter-hedge (or when spoken 'the winter-'edge'), to air in front of the fire. A common sight would be clothes airing on a long wooden rack hoisted high above the kitchen range. Several Askrigg ladies recalled socks and jumpers being aired in the side oven, which gave them a distinctive smell. Elma Banks and Dorothy Baker were childhood friends in Askrigg and

Sheila Fawcett, also known as 'Mrs Knickers', in front of her well stocked stall in Leyburn market square. The fleecy lined liberty bodice is the shorter length with old fashioned suspenders. A top selling line now for the more mature lady who feels the North Yorkshire winters.

recalled conversations at school such as, 'That's your jumper, it smells of ovens.' Or if you got the jumper of the girl whose father was a joiner, 'That's yours, it smells of sawdust!'

***

An enduring childhood memory of mine is putting on a freshly aired liberty bodice still warm from the fire and being burnt by the rubber buttons. This particular item of clothing is worth a slight diversion. Made of cotton and fleecy lined, only those above a certain age will remember a liberty bodice and none of us with any fondness.

Ann Holubecki had to wear a liberty bodice with suspenders sewn on and black stockings as part of the school uniform of Yorebridge Grammar School in Wensleydale. When the rubber buttons perished she thought, 'Oh good that's the end of that,' but mother sewed on some more. When she was finally allowed to discard the loathed garment, it was used as a floorcloth. 'You wasted nothing in those days.'

This garment was unisex and some boys had to wear it. Barry Tinkler of Bishopton remembered a childhood at Great Stainton in the early 1950s. If he had a cold his mother insisted on the following curative measures. A grey paste (in conversation with Barry neither of us could think what this might be) rubbed onto chest, followed by a layer of pink lint, front and back, to keep in the warmth, a vest, then a liberty bodice and finally outdoor clothes. At the age of eight he rebelled and refused to wear either the vest or the liberty bodice but he remembered a fellow sufferer, another boy, who also wore one for much longer.

As an adult I often wondered about the name. Research at the Beamish North of England Open Air Museum, where liberty bodices can still be seen in the draper's shop, revealed they became popular during World War One. Women went out to work and needed less constricting clothing than corsets and stays, hence the name 'liberty'.

***

So with the children bathed, the washing and ironing done, surely a woman could rest awhile – but no. They lived up to the old adage of a woman's work is never done and idle moments were few. Other household chores were just waiting to be done: the pursuit of cleanliness was relentless.

Elbow Grease

—— ❧ ——

'A cobweb i' t' kitchen
An feeat-marks on t' step
Finnd neea wood i' t' yewn
An' neea cooals i' t' skep.'
(yewn – oven, skep – willow basket)

Visitors to North Yorkshire cannot fail to admire its beauties: the hills, rivers and waterfalls of the Dales; the sweeping grandeur of the Moors; the warmth of the people, the good pub food and splendid local beer. Picturesque cottages clustered round ancient churches, stone barns and drystone walls criss-crossing the fellsides, the sheep grazing high on the . . . but I must stop; this is not a travel guide.

For while all this is true, there is a darker, damper side to North Yorkshire. We can do our best to make cottages weatherproof but the driving rain and west wind are always playing with the roof slates, penetrating our porous stone walls: damp is never far away in an old Yorkshire house. Imagine, without the benefit of modern building materials, central heating and double glazing, how difficult it must have been to keep warm and dry.

Roy Kneeshaw of Askrigg allowed me to dip into his grandmother's book of household hints collected over the years. There were many useful snippets of information including, 'to render boots and shoes waterproof in damp weather rub a little mutton suet round the edges of the soles.' However, my eye was caught by a newspaper clipping, 'Reinserted by Request for Damp Walls. Strip off the paper where it is damp. Get a sheet of brown paper, blacklead one side and place the blackened side to the wall and put your wallpaper on top.' Another remedy was to brush the wall with two layers of tar, particularly recommended for damp places round sinks and scullery walls.

Life was a constant battle fought mainly in the kitchen. The parlour was used only for special occasions, often to do with death. It was in this room that the coffin would rest with the lid open for people to come and pay their last respects to the deceased. The kitchen was a much cheerier place, the hub of the house. Life went on round the kitchen range: you cooked, heated water, bathed, ate, aired clothes, ironed, kept warm, gossiped, loved and quarrelled. The kitchen range developed from the late 17th century; made of iron, its gaping maw needed constant filling with coal and wood. No walk was complete without 'sticking', returning with armfuls of twigs and branches to feed the household monster.

The weekly job of blackleading the beast was a filthy job, the smoke and soot coming from the range adding to the burden of housework. Cleaning the chimney was accomplished by thrusting upwards with either a bunch of ling or the branch of a gooseberry bush, or another good flue brush could be made from goose wings. Though out on Blea Moor the railwayman Jack Dawson had a novel way of clearing the chimney, by throwing a hazard warning detonator on the fire which exploded and down came the soot!

Housework was never ending, as Eleanor Dinsdale of Carperby explained to me. 'My family name was Fawcett and as a teenager we lived in Nappa Hall, a house dating from the middle of the 15th century. There were twenty-six rooms and a large family to feed and keep clean. During the War there was Mum and Dad, six children, an old uncle, two friends of my mother's from Sunderland who had been bombed out and later four boy evacuees. There were never less than sixteen sitting down to every meal and we always had a damask starched tablecloth on the table. We baked twenty-three loaves twice a week and Mother baked fresh pies when we needed them, unlike some who would bake for a week and by the end of the week, especially in summer, the pies had got fur coats on!

Monday was washday with over twenty shirts to be washed in the dolly tub. Tuesday we ironed, while Father went to Hawes market. Wednesday we cleaned upstairs. Thursday we baked bread, teacakes, oatcakes and bannocks. Friday we cleaned up all round, and at night time I waited for everyone to go to bed and then I blackleaded the kitchen range and scrubbed the flag floor. Saturday the outside flags were swept and on Sunday it was a day of rest as there was only the

A very old kitchen range in Askrigg belonging to Harold Hammond. One side of the fire is an oven, the other a ten gallon water tank. This range could still be used but it is in a holiday cottage and Harold says people have lost the skill to tend a fire, without setting the chimney alight or burning the carpet.

A kitchen range belonging to Edna Hammond of Askrigg. The reckan is the iron bar hanging from the rannel balk, a beam across the fireplace. The reckan had holes to take hooks for hanging a kettle over the fire. The height of the kettle was adjusted up and down and the reckan bar could be moved from side to side along the rannel balk.

Sunday roast dinner to cook. Then you started all over again . . .'

Even with all this weekly work Spring Cleaning still had to be done. According to Amy Scarr of Bainbridge, downstairs by Easter; upstairs by Whitsuntide. Standards were maintained. In parts of Wensleydale it was quite common to take your carpet for a walk across the fields to freshen it up. This is not as absurd as it sounds. Elma Banks, Denny Minnitt and Dorothy Baker of Askrigg, friends since schooldays, remember taking a corner of the carpet, not always willingly, and setting off across the fields with their mothers, pulling the carpet behind them. This was done when the 'fog' (grass which had just started growing after a first cut) was right and you had to be on the look out for cowpats and sheep droppings. Less energetic forms of carpet cleaning involved sprinkling the carpet with damp tea leaves or torn up strips of wet newspaper and sweeping them up vigorously.

Most farmers' wives had a servant girl living in. They often came from poorer hill farms high up in the Dales. The story goes of one young girl who when asked by the farmer's wife to make a salad, boiled the lettuce! Farms were often supplemented at haytime with Irish labourers. Elma told of Michael who had come to Hawes to be hired for a month for the harvest. He always wore a trilby hat and had a cardboard suitcase and although he slept in the farm outbuildings he ate with the family. Elma remembered him eating plums and taking careful aim, spitting the stones across the room onto the carpet. One assumes that the carpet was taken for another walk after this event.

Not that Elma would have been allowed to get away with that sort of behaviour, especially if the preacher came to tea. Elma admitted that she invariably played up when there were visitors. So under the table Elma's mother kept a clock golf club and if knife and fork were not being properly held, Elma would feel a discreet gentle tap on the legs. Methodist ministers in those days were renowned for their eating abilities. Elma's granny entertained one and on offering him some apple pie, one half of which was cut into pieces the other half left whole, the minister took the uncut half!

Bedrooms were cold, inhospitable places with linoleum or bare floorboards and if you were lucky a rag rug by the side of the bed. Although bedrooms had fireplaces, in North Yorkshire where folk have grown hardy, the fire was lit only if you were at death's door. It was an indication of how gravely ill you were and people remarked in hushed tones, 'She's lit a fire for him.' You knew he was not long for this world.

Stone hot water bottles were used to lift the chill as you slid between the sheets but Blanche Young of Harmby Women's Institute wrapped the warm shelves of the oven and took them to bed with her. A washstand with basin and jug was considered a luxury and you certainly did not linger over your strip wash in winter. Audrey Bailey of Thoralby lived on her parents' farm in Caldwell. She was fifteen before they got electricity and she remembered washing in a basin in the bedroom and then taking the water downstairs in the slop bucket. Unfortunately she fell down the stairs one time while carrying a full slop bucket; thank goodness it was not anything worse. Audrey recalled hard but happy times: 'the fun you could get out of a pig's bladder!'

Children were certainly expected to do their share of the household tasks and often they were lumbered with the ones nobody else wanted to do. You were given a huge apron for Christmas, generally about the age of nine, and this was a signal that you were old enough to help. Imagine today's children if they found an apron in their Christmas stocking!

***

One of the most unpleasant jobs around the house must have been the morning ritual of emptying the chamber pot. My mother only started smoking in her thirties when grandfather, who was poorly, came to live with us. He could not make it across the landing to our bathroom and required a nightly chamber pot. 'A cigarette helped,' she declared.

Irene Stacey of Richmond will never forget her precise instructions. 'It was my job as a young girl living on an Uncle's farm to empty the chamber pots each day. I took a bucket of clean water upstairs with me (although that farmhouse had a bath and washbasin), I carefully carried all the chamber pots, one by one into the bathroom. I emptied the first into the second and then put water into the first. I emptied the third into the fourth and put water into the third. There were usually four potties to be emptied. By then the water was almost used, so I could empty the urine into the bucket, use the water from the first and third to cleanse the second and fourth and so all were clean and could be returned under their respective beds. I then carried the full bucket downstairs and emptied those contents down a drain, filling the bucket

A washstand dating from between 1790 and 1800. With all the carrying and emptying that went on it is a wonder that any of the original china survived. Later washstands were rectangular, often with a mirror at the back.

A Victorian washbasin, jug and soap dish for use in the bedroom.

with fresh water and emptying that water down the drain and returning the bucket to its home under the stairs. I did this job every day and I started when I was nine and threequarter years, continuing until I was almost twelve.'

In one of her published short stories Irene wrote of the additional burden at haytime. 'I also had the job of emptying the Irishmen's chamber pots when they slept in a loft above the kitchen. I had to climb and descend a ladder (wide and safe but a ladder none the less) and throughout the whole operation, either upstairs in the farm or in haytime, I had not to spill a single drop.'

Gwen Welton had to do chores on the farm at Ellerbeck near Northallerton. 'We had chamber pots under the beds which had to be emptied before I left for school. My younger brother had to help in the house as well. One day he had emptied the pots and rinsed them (we took two buckets upstairs, one empty one, the other with hot water in) and as he was carrying two of the pots back he was swinging them from back to front but this one time they crashed together and broke. Yes, he cop't it from our father!'

As household objects chamber pots were cherished, after all they saved you from the long walk down the path to the privy on a cold, dark night. Tucked under the bed out of sight they were made of earthenware or china with delicate designs of birds and flowers. As with anything connected with 'bodily functions' euphemisms abounded. From the 'pysse potte' of earlier times through to 'jerry' (from jeroboam – a large bottle), the 'gazunder', 'po', 'potty', no bedroom was complete without one.

Raymond Jones of Great Burdon has a theory why so many chamber pots were smashed or cracked and he may well be right. When beds were made of iron or brass they were regularly taken to pieces to clean. The iron struts across the base were not always put back securely. His parents after just such a spring cleaning job, got into bed and they and the bed came crashing down, smashing the chamber pot underneath.

Indeed it was felt by some to be a wise precaution to cover the contents of the chamber pot, as the steam from the urine rusted the bedsprings!

Nothing was wasted. Urine from the chamber pot went onto the midden and from there onto the garden. Kathy Fawcett of Bedale knew of an old lady in Bainbridge who always emptied her chamber pot straight over the rhubarb and gooseberries. 'She used to offer them to me saying, "They're nice an' juicy now." I always declined. I've always doubted gooseberries.'

Several people have vouched for the efficacy of urine as a cure for chilblains, not taken internally of course, but the offending part dipped into the pot. Another certain cure, this time for warts, was to keep dabbing the wart with urine.

The contents of the chamber pot could be put into the final rinse for blankets, to make them soft and fluffy! In the West Riding textile mills, urine was used commercially and the 'lant', as it was called, was collected from willing householders by a carter often with the sobriquet 'Piss' added to his name. Urine was excellent for removing stains and grease and some used it as a beauty treatment to rinse their faces. However, I can imagine these will be household hints from yesteryear that you will not be anxious to try.

Just part of the chamber pot collection to be viewed at Newby Hall. The two-handled ones must have made carrying and emptying much safer. (By kind permission of The Newby Hall Estate)

Muck

'There is usually an evident desire to keep clean and neat as possible, even under circumstances, the most unfavourable to personal and domestic cleanliness.' Sanitary sub committee of York 1844.

In this book we are never far from defecatory matters. You may wish it otherwise but we cannot turn aside: we must be thorough. In the house the kitchen range ruled with its unceasing need for fuel; in the garden the privy and its contents were equally demanding. Women did their best to keep the privy sweet. An early form of air freshener was a saucer containing Dettol and water. Others put bunches of wild flowers on the window sill and 'improving' texts on the wall. The seat and floor had to be scrubbed, the walls regularly painted with quicklime, a weekly supply of paper be provided and the contents disposed of thoughtfully. The latter job was usually done by any male in the house who could be coerced into taking up his shovel: the females were responsible for the other chores.

Mrs Carr during her childhood in Winterburn had many jobs to do on a Saturday morning including cleaning the windows, scrubbing the two-holer seat with soda and then the 'flags' with a besom brush and finally cutting the *Craven Herald* into squares to be hung on a nail for use as lavatory paper. However, it was granddad's job to fork out the privy at the back, mix in the ash from the fire and from there spread the nourishing mixture onto the land.

That the contents of the privy, suitably mixed with ashes, could add to the fertility of the soil is in no doubt. Mrs Garbutt of Bedale proved the point that 'where there's muck there's brass'. She spent her childhood in the 1930s at Great Smeaton. 'The school caretaker used the contents of the school privies to enhance his vegetable patch. He grew the biggest prize winning cabbages and the best leeks in the area.

The three-holer privy belonging to a former vicarage on the Yorkshire/Durham border was cleared from the back onto the midden, discreetly hidden by a wall at the edge of the field. The small door opened onto the midden from the garden side through which servants disposed of kitchen waste and the contents of the chamber pots.

Any "waste" left over would be sold to other gardeners – a bucketful for a pint of beer.' He was very successful at this trading, even at times too successful. 'After coming out of the pub I helped him by holding his bike while he got onto it. We pushed him off and he would go down the hill for half a mile – until he fell off at his front door. He would give a halfpence for this service or one penny on a good day. I always had money to lend to my older brother, so he could buy sweets for his girlfriend, or take her to the pictures in Darlington. He never did pay me back!'

Whilst researching this subject I found that many Dalesfolk spoke in awe of the privies at Nappa Hall in Wensleydale. Eleanor Dinsdale of Carperby lived there as a young woman with her parents and large family, increased because of wartime by several evacuees. As befitted such an establishment the privies were many and superior. Eleanor

Ann Holubecki sharing a privy memory with Sheila Scarr who now lives in Ann's childhood home near Askrigg. Ann used to drum her heels against the side of this two-holer privy to frighten away any lurking creatures. When the privy was getting full it was cleared through the hole at the back by a long fork onto the midden in the field behind.

recalled, ' The privy block had a three-holer for the women and with another entrance a two-holer for the men. Our bachelor uncles did not always spend their clothes coupons and when there was a family wedding, the girls would hunt for all the spare coupons. We found some that were out of date and hung them in the privy as a joke.

'Everyone kept to their own gender privies. We had a farmworker staying in the house and he was taken ill during the night. To get to the privies from his bedroom, he had to go down four flights of eight stairs to get to outside and then up some steps and then a twenty yard slope. He was in such a rush that he used the ladies privy but in the morning he apologised. "I was that bad last night, I had to use the women's – I hope you don't mind." We always referred to a visit to the privy as "going up the slope".

'You needed a raincoat on a wet night but your troubles were not over when you arrived, as the back of the privy faced west. (Author's note: the prevailing wind in Wensleydale is west, strong and often.) When it was windy you had to be careful when you lifted the lid, otherwise the paper inside was liable to blow up and out. There was a slate over the hole at the back but it was not entirely windproof. It was raked out regularly and mixed with ash, whoever did it was allowed a whisky afterwards.'

You were very fortunate if nature could help you with your disposal. The streams and becks of North Yorkshire have not always run so clear. It was tempting to build your privy close to running water. A particularly terrifying one belonged to Kathy Fawcett's aunt and uncle at Aysgarth Falls. Anyone who has visited this beauty spot knows that the river Ure in full flood is a magnificent sight; the mighty waters surging and thundering over the limestone terraces. Kathy's uncle was manager of Yore Mills at Aysgarth Falls and their privies were across the road, balanced precariously on the steep side of the river at the Upper Falls. Quite understandably, Kathy had to be led by the hand to use this privy, as she was terrified of falling in the river and being swept to her death.

Tom Peacock of Darlington was born and bred in Swaledale and told me of his maternal grandparents who lived in Arkengarthdale, where grandfather worked the mill. Tom's mother was one of thirteen born there. The stream was diverted for working the grindstone and then diverted back again to flow under the two-holer built over the stream.

A single-holer at West Witton. The contents were mixed with ashes, and the garden when the present owner went there in the 1960s was one huge ashpit.

A two-holer at Redmire. (Photograph Ann Holubecki)

A three-holer behind a late 18th century house in Sand Hutton. The smaller, lower hole was for a child.

This afforded instant disposal; it was just a pity that the stream ran down to the back of the village school. Tom retracing his family roots felt obliged to sit on the whitewashed two-holer, where so many of his family had passed idle moments.

Several members of the Gayle Ladies Club were very revealing on the subject of privy clearing. This delightful little village above Hawes has Duerley Beck running through. Right on the beckside were four privies shared by several families. The men took it in turns to empty the privies with a bucket onto the fields, although whether the beck was ever used to cut corners is lost now in the mists of time. Many soldiers were stationed in Gayle during the Second World War and one of the ladies told of her father walking in the dark carrying the contents of the privy to empty onto the field. A soldier on guard duty shouted, 'Who goes there?' Father replied, 'The shit house emptier.' They let him through pretty quickly!

Not everyone had such instant means at their disposal and often in villages the privy would be emptied by a carter, who would take it to a local farmer to be mixed with the farm muck and then spread onto the fields. A story I heard from several sources concerned an old lady of Askrigg, the contents of whose privy was collected by the local carter. He set off with his wheelbarrow to deliver but no farmer would take it. The carter had to return to Askrigg saying to the old lady, 'Nay, nobody wants thee muck,' and promptly dumped the stuff from whence it came – back in the privy! On hearing this story I was intrigued. Why would they not take it? Was there a vendetta against the old woman? Had she upset a farmer or someone in the village? When enquiring further of longstanding locals, the consensus of opinion was that the contents of her privy had been rejected by the farmers, not because of any quarrel, but more a question of the 'quality' of the product.

Some towns and villages had well organised systems of emptying the privies and John King of Romanby liked nothing more than to help out. 'I first started helping out on a local farm in 1944 when I was a young lad. The disposal of the contents of the privies of Brompton near Northallerton was privately run by a farmer. The farmer paid me sixpence for helping out, in particular with the horse that pulled the open cart. Saturday morning I would be there and it was my job to say "drive on" to the horse, which always knew where to stop. We started at the Waterend and when the cart was full we drove the two miles back to Northallerton and spread our collection at the side of the tip, just outside Yafforth Road. We used to sing the old songs as we went along and treat ourselves to fish and chips from the shop after we had dumped the stuff; no matter the state of our hands. In an effort at hygiene the council told us to "sheet up", that is cover the contents of our cart, because we passed the Maternity Hospital. During the week when I couldn't be there the farm men went round the rest of the village houses in Brompton emptying the slop bins supplied by the council into a horsedrawn metal container.'

Further back in time the state of the middens in York aptly demonstrate the problems of disposal. The sweetness of the air in the countryside beyond the city walls was in sharp contrast to what could be breathed in amidst its ancient streets and alleyways. The tourists who flock to admire the grandeur of York Minster, the mediaeval churches, the historic buildings and museums little realise that if they had visited in earlier times, they stood a strong chance of catching something nasty and potentially lethal. Pestilence and disease were rife, especially in the summer months, whilst in winter there was always the problem of flooding; a small thought perhaps for when you next visit this charming city.

A report prepared by T. Laycock MD, Physician to the York Dispensary, dated 1844 makes grim reading. 'The houses of the higher classes, and all the more respectable houses recently built have water closets which empty into drains or cesspools. In the newly built ranges of cottage tenements, one privy is thought appropriate for four, eight, twelve or even fourteen families. The position of the privy is selected evidently without any reference to the health or comfort of the inhabitants.'

Privies frequently flooded in wet weather and generally spilt all over the place and none of this was helped by the fact that many cottages had pigsties, hen roosts and cow houses attached to them. The courts and alleys were cleared by 'appointed scavengers' and the report goes on. 'The night soil is retained, giving off its impurities until a sufficient quantity is accumulated, when it is removed from the yard during the night in barrows and put into the streets; from thence it is carted away to large dung hills within the city. There is an immense heap of this kind at the side of the river Foss, close by Layerthorpe bridge, and the inhabitants all around complain loudly of the stench.'

However, even here someone could make a profit. What might be muck to some was liquid gold to another. The night soil of the city was sold to the owners of these dung hills who were known as 'manure merchants'. It was calculated that a load and a half was taken from each house annually. Plenty of raw material there for a flourishing entrepreneur.

Other Unmentionables

'Cut to a precise size with a hole thrust into the top and fed with string, some made interesting reading. I often noticed menfolk in there far longer than the females.' Irene Stacey.

I have already alluded, albeit briefly, to that other major household task: ensuring a constant supply of paper for use in the privy. The history of bottom wiping is long and fascinating, although probably not one to which you have given much thought.

Briefly, the Romans used a stick with a sponge on the end, washed it in salt water and then placed it back on the ledge ready for the next person to use. This gave us the expression, still used today, 'to get hold of the wrong end of the stick!' The British favoured a curved stick, I can only assume on account of laziness, so we did not have to bend round quite so much, and our stick had a bunch of hay on the end. Monks wasted nothing and used cut up dirty old habits. Ordinary people availed themselves of flat, smooth stones, damp moss, bunches of herbs, straw and dock leaves.

Rolls of lavatory paper were available from 1880 onwards but for most people a newspaper square was the favoured wipe. Clear favourites emerge. The *Radio Times* was strong and each page cut up nicely into four pieces. The *Daily Mail* gave an awfully good wipe as the print did not come off. Other newspapers favoured were the *Daily Herald*, the *News of the World*, the *Darlington and Stockton Times*, the *Yorkshire Post* and the *Beano*. Amongst the farming community of North Yorkshire there was always the *Farmers Weekly* to read and then use.

Nonconformity has always been strong in the Dales and one lady told me of an aunt who always used the *Methodist Recorder*. However, the *Christian Herald* was favoured in Gayle. The Hopper family of

This illustration shows a Roman military latrine with the sponge 'poo sticks' in a bowl in the centre. The large trough contained salt water.

Wensleydale made full use of an old telephone directory, by just tearing off a page as and when required. Members of the family recall that whilst it was only fairly soft, it was a great improvement on newspaper.

Ingenuity knew no bounds as the soft tissue paper of old dress patterns and the paper wrapped round bread and oranges all found their way to the back of the privy door. Some farmers' daughters were very fortunate as they had access to tissue paper that separated the sile pads used for straining milk, a nice, soft alternative. However, for sheer style you could not beat the family of Shirley Bell of Belmont Women's Institute. Her father was farm manager in the late 1930s on the Ripley Estate near Harrogate. Her mother Mrs Kay used to cut up the newspaper squares with dressmaker's crimping shears, so that each sheet had a lovely crimped edge. Standards had to be kept up, living so near the Big House.

***

Yorkshire people may have a reputation for plain speaking but when it came to their privies they were as fond of euphemisms as any from the Home Counties. Spades were not always called spades. There were several favourite northern alternatives to the word 'privy', their derivation hidden in the mists of sanitation history. 'Netty' could date back to when the Romans were here as the Italian 'gabinetti' means a row of toilets. 'Petty' came from the French 'petit' meaning small. 'Nessy' was a shortened form of 'the necessary house.'

'The Necessary' needed to be named in formal documents as shown from this extract from an Askrigg will dated 28th February 1800. 'To my son William . . . the Dwellinghouse in Skellgill West of that wherein I now live with the garden and Appurtenances . . . also the West part of Hargill when divided from the North East Corner of the Necessary to the Ash Tree or Bush on the West Side of the Wath crossing the Beck . . .

'To my daughter Sarah . . . the Dwelling House, Stable, Garden and Necessary in Skellgill wherein I now live. William shall have the Previlege [sic] of a Cart Road . . . at all times of the year when the grass is not up . . . the Cart Road shall be from the Necessary to and through the Wath.' A man who was leaving nothing to chance.

All families had their favourite little sayings. Some of my favourites collected in Yorkshire include:

The Palace of Varieties
The Houses of Parliament (on account of the long sittings)
Midden'ole
I have to go and shake my lettuce
Going for a sweet pea
Making a deposit at the bank
Have you been to the watery?
Going for a pony (rhyming slang – pony and trap!)
Going for a bubble
Going up the slope

The George Inn in the tiny hamlet of Hubberholme in Upper Wharfedale favours a farming theme – Ewes and Tups. A town dwelling friend of mine from the south faced with the two doors demanded to know which one was she?

Barbara Brown of Masham Women's Institute attended the College of Ripon and York St John in Ripon where the students would use a theological euphemism, 'Going to Moab'. For those readers needing an explanation you will find in Psalm 108, verse 9 'Moab is my washpot' – a suitable insult as 'washpot' has been euphemistically translated. The Israelites were frequently at war with the Moabites.

You would think the medical profession could deal in plain speaking, but no. As a child in hospital I was asked by a nurse if I had 'opened my bowels'. I did not have a clue what she was talking about.

John King of Romanby was an in-patient in the mid 1940s at a sanatorium in Thornton Rust for fresh air treatment. Every night a nurse would ask, 'Have you had a mark?' and it went into a book. Even if you had not 'been' you still said you had, otherwise you got a double dose of syrup of figs. John and a few others developed a special skill of keeping the syrup in the mouth without swallowing. He could be given the dreaded dose, walk fifty yards from the dining room, up the back stairs and along a corridor to the bathroom and there spit the horrid stuff out. 'One of the nurses knew we did it and she would make us stand there and swallow.'

Ann Coates of Thirsk kindly sent me a copy of a letter she had received in 1952 from Major J. Fairfax-Blakeborough MC, a well known writer on country pursuits, hunting and the Turf. He had a huge list of publications to his name and I am ashamed to admit I have not read any. Just selecting one at random from the list, *The Life of H.W. Selby Lowndes, M.F.H.*, will give you an indication of his interests. For some reason Ann had felt moved to write to the great man on the subject of her 'petty' and he found time to reply with a very agreeable letter, delicately worded: 'Your commodious sociable garden convenience was quite common fifty years ago. The first I remember was at Paradise Farm at Guisborough at which a great aunt of mine lived. Not only was provision made for Father Bear, Mrs Bear and little Bear but I recall a pile of literature to entertain the constipated. She always sensed when we were "going" and would call out to us;

> "To keep that little City sweet
> Open the door and close the seat." '

And Now For Something Superior

———— ❧ ————

'Much knowledge may be obtained by a good housewife observing how things are managed in well-regulated families.' A 1930 self help book.

Time to 'name drop' and consider bathroom improvements, the upper class and even royalty, not that these three subjects were necessarily synonymous. Having left the old millennium and embarked on the new it has been a popular item on regional television and in newspapers to consider who has been the Yorkshireman or woman who has contributed most to the common good, or as some people might put it 'Top Tykes'.

Forget the transitory glories of leather on willow or those who play with funny shaped balls and let us consider a more solid achievement. Top of my list would be the Yorkshireman Captain James Cook who knew all about the importance of hygiene and eating fresh fruit to keep your ship's crew healthy. His attention to detail resulted in Britain acquiring the Australasian territories, which in turn allowed us to offload our 'undesirables' and from this cultural melting pot we acquired Foster's lager, Rolf Harris and various daytime 'soap operas'.

Captain Cook's achievement was great but there was another up there in the pantheon of great Yorkshiremen: one who eased the burden of women and released men from the purgatory of the privy or 'shittush' shovel. I write of Thomas Crapper, a remarkable sanitary engineer and one whose very name has passed into the English language. Often used as a derogatory adjective, those who take his name in vain have no understanding of this great man and his profound effect on our bathrooms.

He was born in Thorne near Doncaster in 1837 and although this is South Yorkshire, he is too important a figure to leave out on a mere question of geography. He came of humble stock and a large family and left home at the age of eleven to walk to London. I imagine he was too poor to get there any other way, rather than practising Yorkshire thrift. In London he found work with a master plumber in Chelsea and never looked back, for in 1861 he set up his own business as 'Manufacturing Sanitary Engineers'. It was just at the right time as the great and the good, parliamentary legislators and royalty were at last taking an interest in their sewage.

Thomas Crapper did not invent the water closet but he was certainly one of those responsible for perfecting it. Another Yorkshireman, Joseph Bramah, in the 18th century had gone before with his hinged valve and countless others had tried to overcome the problem of flush, water wastage and smell. Crapper worked long and hard on the strength of his flush mechanism and his success was rewarded by the patronage of royalty. However, his inventions did not stop with the Valveless Waste Preventer; he improved the design of the ordinary household drain and was much concerned with adequate ventilation. He died in 1910, venerated within the plumbing fraternity but an unsung hero to the rest of the population whose bathrooms he worked so hard to improve. Let us indeed 'praise famous men', particularly this Yorkshireman.

***

On the whole royal personages have not chosen to make their homes in North Yorkshire. The crowded charms of Gloucestershire and the M4, the windswept flatness of Norfolk or even the damp and midges of Scotland in August are preferred to our glorious countryside. A quick visit for some grouse shooting or the cutting of a ribbon is about all we can expect. However, there may be a reason for this reluctance and the Palace should be informed that the county's drains are as good as anywhere in the country.

The course of history nearly changed on a royal visit to North Yorkshire. The Prince of Wales, later to become Edward VII, visited Scarborough in 1871 and almost died, having caught typhoid while staying with the Countess of Londesborough at Londesborough Lodge.

Her drains were the cause. Illnesses like this were no respecter of persons; dear Prince Albert had been carried off ten years earlier by the same disease but as that was in Windsor we could not possibly be held responsible.

Back in the 15th century Richard III thought North Yorkshire was a cracking place to live. Middleham was the 'Windsor of the North' and regarded as his favourite residence. However, go further back to 1400 and another Richard, the second one, met a very nasty end involving a red hot poker in Pontefract Castle. Surely it is time to let bygones be bygones and forgive these inhospitable ways.

We did have one queen who spent time here, albeit reluctantly. Mary Queen of Scots was detained 'at Her Majesty's Pleasure' for six months from 13th July 1568 under the protective custody of the ninth Baron Scope in his magnificent Bolton Castle. At the time she probably wished herself elsewhere and failed to appreciate the splendid sweeping views of Wensleydale from her apartments. One of the finest preserved castles in the country, Bolton Castle is open to the public and all visitors must be impressed by its position and grandeur dominating the surrounding countryside.

It was an ideal spot to put a queen who was becoming a bit of a nuisance but they did their best to make her stay pleasant. Her Majesty used the Solar, a small sitting room looking south over the gardens and Pen Hill beyond. She requested more rugs as she found the floors rather cold but with rugs, tapestries and a good fire this room would have been very comfortable. Her every need, apart from freedom, was catered for. A narrow passage leads off the Solar to the garderobe with washbasin and a place for the water jug. The garderobe was built over a chute which dropped down into a pit which was cleared every six months.

The building of Bolton Castle was started in 1379 and was extremely sophisticated for its day. The original contract stipulated that each private apartment must have a privée en suite and the cess pits under the garderobes were still in use in Victorian times. Will today's plumbing last as long?

Ann Holubecki remembers great celebrations at Bolton Castle for the Festival of Britain in 1951. Everyone dressed in the costumes of Elizabeth I and there were tableaux and plays in all the rooms. Ann and her two sisters, who were dressed as serving maids, decided to go

Magnificent Bolton Castle near Leyburn in Wensleydale, open to the public. The south facing wall had water chutes and garderobes draining downhill away from the castle. (Photograph Ann Holubecki by kind permission of Bolton Castle)

The privy and washing place off the Solar at Bolton Castle. As used by Mary Queen of Scots? (By kind permission of Bolton Castle)

for absolute authenticity and use the garderobes. They soon discovered that there was the most terrific wind whistling up the long drop and all Ann's attempts at throwing a piece of paper down the chute came to naught as it just flew back up again. Perhaps Mary Queen of Scots was not so comfortable after all.

***

Sanitation and bathroom reform moved slowly, especially among the upper classes; the working classes could not look to them for guidance. Life in a big Country House was cold, draughty and uncomfortable. Food was rarely hot on account of the great distance between dining room and kitchen. The table may have looked sumptuous as appearance was everything, but the chances were the cook, housekeeper and butler below stairs were eating hotter, fresher food than their masters.

In the late 18th century bath tubs appeared in some of the grander houses, although the water was seldom hot or the system even working and on turning the tap you were more likely to get dead earwigs and bluebottles than hot water. The hip bath in front of the fire was much preferred and the only difference between the Master and the humble Dalesman was that one would bathe in the bedroom and the other in the kitchen. Both were seeking warmth.

We have an image of Victorian ladies with the vapours, reclining on a chaise longue feeling slightly unwell. We may dismiss them as raging hypochondriacs but the chances were that the drains and the noxious fumes seeping back from them through the house were indeed the cause of their illnesses. Early water closets often suffered from a build up of methane gas and many a Victorian gentleman has withdrawn to the smallest room after dinner, lit a cigar and met with more than he bargained for . . .

However, there was one rather grand Edwardian house in North Yorkshire that had the most advanced water system and where everything was the most comfortable and modern available – even central heating in the corridors and main reception rooms!

Sion Hill Hall at Kirby Wiske, near Thirsk, is a magnificent example of the last of the Country Houses to be built before the Great War. There had been houses on the site since 1209 but by the time Percy

Sylvia Gadsby at Sion Hill Hall with a cast iron, white enamelled bath of considerable proportions – 21 inches deep and nearly 7 feet long. The bell push in the wall above the bath summoned the maid. (By kind permission of the Board of Trustees Sion Hill Hall)

The Hellyer Optimus [G] – an improved valve closet, still working, at Sion Hill Hall. The complex system is concealed in a throne-like casing with mahogany seat, the strong flush activated by an upward pull of the handle. Stevens Hellyer was a Victorian plumber, writer and agitator for sanitary reform. (By kind permission of the Board of Trustees Sion Hill Hall)

Stancliffe bought the Georgian mansion from the Lascelles family in 1911, it was in such poor condition that it was fit only to be pulled down. There was no drinking water inside the house and the well which supplied the only potable water was pumped dry in twenty minutes.

The Stancliffes had made their wealth in the brewing industry and added to his wife Ethel's money, Stancliffe could afford to have the best. He employed the York architect Walter H. Brierley, known as 'The Lutyens of the North', to build the house for him. Not that the architect had a completely free hand as Mr Stancliffe kept a tight control on finances and paid minute attention to every detail.

After Mr Stancliffe died the Hall and estate were bought by Mr H.W. Mawer, an astute businessman and avid collector of antiques. It is his collection of beautiful objects that you can see in the rooms that can be viewed by the public.

Originally the water for the house was collected in two 15,000 gallon cisterns under the forecourt. Rainwater from the roof went to one and well water to the other, this was then pumped up into four very large tanks situated in a specially strengthened roof space and fed back into the house by gravity. A notice indicating 'Hard Water to Servants Quarters' and 'Soft Water to the House' was affixed to the tanks. However, the servants at Sion Hill were well treated and had, for that time, the exquisite luxury of a large plumbed in bath, washbasin, flush toilet and part central heating to their quarters, this when other far grander establishments would have been breaking the ice on the water in their bedroom washstands in winter.

An enjoyable afternoon was spent examining the plumbing with Tom Gadsby, who is a member of the Board of Trustees of the H.W. Mawer Trust which administers the Hall, and his wife Sylvia, the Hon Secretary, who with the Resident Trustee Michael Mallaby help to look after this lovely house. Everything was of the finest quality with deep cast iron baths, generous sized washbasins, fine nickel plated fittings, all made by the top names of the day: Doulton of London and Paisley, Dent and Hellyer Ltd, and Shanks of Barrhead, Scotland.

The house is open to the public from April to the end of September and although I have a preference for bathrooms, I suspect most visitors come to admire the fine porcelain, paintings, clocks and furniture displayed in a welcoming setting.

I have written previously about the humble chamber pot and its place under the beds of the working class but it was an object that crossed the barriers of class and was highly regarded for its convenience in the homes of the rich.

In ruder, rougher times no one bothered to conceal a chamber pot. Thankfully ideas of decency developed until by the 18th century the more high toned houses had chamber pots under the bed, hidden from view by a valance round the bed or in a cabinet called a night table for 'the accidental occasions of the night'. A commode was a hiding place for a chamber pot, often in a chair or steps which also aided the ascent into a high feather bed.

Regency times saw elegant sideboards in the dining rooms of the rich with a cupboard at one end for the chamber pot or a recess containing a pot, behind a window shutter, all for the use of gentlemen after dinner; the ladies had to go elsewhere. Hiding the pot was all very well but often in the grander house, with the total reliance on servants for everything, its presence could still be detected, when those

The exquisite Victorian 'Motto' bedroom at Newby Hall. The mottoes were painted by Lady Mary Vyner in 1857 and the bath translates as 'without stain' and the water can as 'a trifle'. (By kind permission of The Newby Hall Estate)

responsible for emptying were dilatory in their duties. It was not all sweetness up at the Big House.

There are many fine Country Houses in North Yorkshire and one of the most splendid must be Newby Hall just outside Ripon. It is a mecca for gardeners and those interested in garden design. The plantings are voluptuous with roses, herbaceous borders, the rock garden and much more. The house is grand and elegant with furnishings of great taste all displayed to advantage for the enjoyment of visitors. However, a tour of the house reveals a little gem of a room containing a collection of objects without equal: the Newby Hall Chamber Pot Room or the 'Po Room'.

The collection was amassed by Robert de Grey Vyner on his travels in Europe and the Far East. The collection spans from rough 16th century peasant ware to 18th and 19th century fine china. Home grown pots in Sunderland lustre ware and Leeds Creamware, fine Chinese porcelain, elegant monogrammed bourdaloues for ladies, pots with frogs inside, others with leering faces, many with saucy rhymes, all displayed with great style.

(By kind permission of The Newby Hall Estate)

Some 'saucy' chamber pots from the Newby Hall Collection. What with leering faces, frogs and a disconcerting eye, could anyone bear to use these? (By kind permission of The Newby Hall Estate)

This remarkable collection has even been favoured by royalty. Queen Mary on a visit to Newby Hall, belying her rather forbidding and regal exterior, declared the chamber pot collection to be truly unique! One can only wonder what Her Majesty made of such rhymes as:

> Dear Mary don' you see,
> Hand it over unto me.

> Pick me up and use me well
> And what I see I will never tell.

> For a kiss I'll hand you this.

Not probably what she was used to!

Taking the Waters

———— ❧ ————

'They prove highly beneficial in most forms of indigestion with its usual accompaniments: Constipation, Flatulence and Acidity.' A recommendation for the Harrogate sulphur waters, 1875.

Harrogate has been attracting visitors for four hundred years. A former spa town that developed into a major conference centre with elegant hotels, shops and tea rooms, the Valley Gardens, the Mercer Art Gallery, Turkish Baths and the magnificent 200 acres of The Stray. In its heyday as a spa town this was where the Yorkshire middle classes came to cure their aches and pains, mixing with European royalty, politicians, celebrities, the famous and the infamous. People from the Dales too would make the journey into town in search of relief from rheumatism.

The Royal Pump Room Museum, built over the site of the strongest sulphur spring in England, tells the history of Harrogate as a spa town. The word 'museum' can conjure up cavernous halls of dusty exhibits housed in glass cases, watched over by steely eyed attendants – but not this one. Small, friendly, a 'bite-sized' museum; one to pop into for an hour on a wet afternoon. The Pump Room was the obvious place to visit to find out more about the liquid that a doctor in 1626 claimed, 'cheereth and reviveth the spirits, strengtheneth the stomache, causeth good and quick appetite and furthereth digestion.' This must be some water!

The Tewitt Well was first discovered in High Harrogate as far back as 1571 by William Slingsby of Bilton Park and was promoted by him as having medicinal and health giving properties. The Harrogate tourist industry was born.

There are eighty-eight springs, of which sixteen could be used medicinally, within a radius of two miles of Harrogate town centre so it was not surprising that others jumped on the bandwagon of what would turn out to be 'a nice little earner'. With the discovery of another chalybeate or iron spring, the John Well in 1631, there was no looking back. Hotels, lodging houses, shops all sprang up to cater for those who came looking for good health and cures in the Harrogate waters.

A male visitor could expect a warm welcome, in the form of an early morning visit from certain females, bearing pots of the medicinal water. A writer of the time was not impressed with the ladies' fair charms: 'but to tell you the truth they fell short of that, for their faces did shine like bacon rind; and for beauty may vie with an old Bath guide's ass.'

Operations expanded with the discovery in 1695 of Low Harrogate's sulphur well, a strong saline sulphur, descriptively known as 'The Stinking Spaw'. The smell of sulphur was exceptionally strong and pungent but people flocked to it, believing, as we still do today, that if it tastes nasty it must be doing some good. 'The Stinking Spaw' proved popular in the curing of rheumatism, gout, digestive ailments and skin disease – a very impressive list.

It is still possible to drink the sulphur water in the Royal Pump Room Museum. The sulphur well is down in the basement and after the museum was restored in 1987 it is now behind glass. The fumes are such that neither the building nor the exhibits could stand up to them! Small thimbleful glasses of the water are available and I was warned not to sniff at it – as you might a fine wine – but to knock it back in one shot. Ignoring the advice I sniffed and regretted it as a powerful smell redolent of rotting eggs cleared my long blocked sinuses. Swallowing was a distasteful business.

You are not of course remotely interested in the state of my sinuses and I mention them only to show to what lengths people would go. Celia Fiennes, an unusual gentlewoman who travelled throughout England in the late 17th century, wrote in her diary of her visit to the 'Stinking Well' in 1697. Her horse would not go near the water for the smell but she managed to down a quart of the stuff on two successive days. Later on in the 18th century two pints a day was considered a more reasonable amount. A heroic achievement.

By the 18th century facilities round the well-heads had become more sophisticated. The spa town was growing and sounds rather jolly:

The sulphur well with Chippendale canopy in Low Harrogate, 1829. (By kind permission of Harrogate Museums and Art Gallery Service)

'the Rendezvous of wantoness and not seldom of mad Frolicks.' If you did not want to venture too near the smell or the crush of people, a well woman would bring the water to you. The most famous of these was Betty Lupton who lived from 1760 to 1843. Known as the 'Queen of the Wells' she dispensed sulphur water for sixty years, right up to a year before her death. We can only assume that her sense of smell was either non existent or ruined, but it did her no harm, judging from her longevity.

The Royal Pump Room Museum has an extract on display from *Sketches of Harrogate by a Citizen of the World 1841*, giving us a glimpse of life round the sulphur well. 'Most of the visitors are early risers. At Seven o' Clock or soon after, they flock to the Old Sulphur Well, the Waters of which are distributed by some 8 or 10 nymphs whose personal attractions are not calculated to make one insensible to the nauseous flavour of the draught they bestow. The lady paramount of the fount is an old dame, styled indifferently "Old Betty" and "The Queen of Harrogate" over whose head some eighty summers have passed without diminishing her activity or garrulity. She is a privileged person, and dispenses the waters and quips and quodlibets with equal liberality.'

You not only drank the water but you could bathe in it as well, 'in a tub eight feet long, the water warmed as hot as it is well bearable.' You soaked from ten to thirty minutes depending how long the attendant thought 'your Constitution will bear.' One visitor was so amazed by the experience that he described it in verse:

'Astonished I saw when I came to my doffing
A tub of hot water made just like a coffin,
In which the good woman who attended the bath
Declar'd I must lie down as straight as a lath,
Just keeping my face above water, that so
I might better inhale the fine fumes from below.'

Sweating followed on, wrapped up in a blanket bed, although by the late 1700s Harrogate hygiene was such that the practice of dozens of people continually using the same sweating bed was known not to be a good idea. Originally water for bathing was brought to your lodgings but as more visitors flocked to the town special bathing establishments were built.

The coming of the railways to Harrogate in the 1840s heralded a golden age for the spa town. In 1842 the Pump Room was built and the rich and fashionable could drink their water in style and comfort. There was a prescribed daily routine and a stay in Harrogate of three weeks was considered necessary for the treatments to work, followed by a visit to the seaside (were they in league with Scarborough?).

The day always started early at 7 am with a trip to the Pump Room for the first tumbler of water with the rest of the day a continuous round of pleasure: promenading, listening to the band, drinking more water, eating, shopping, bathing, drinking more water, reading, letter writing, driving, walking, cycling, golfing, a concert, until you finally dropped into bed at 10 pm.

The Royal Baths were opened by HRH The Duke of Cambridge in 1897, offering the most advanced hydrotherapy to match any European spa town. There were seventy-seven rich and various treatments to choose from with strange sounding names: the Harrogate Carbonic Acid Bath, the Greville Electric Hot Air Bath, the Sitz Bath, Peat Baths, Needle Baths, the Berthe Douche, Vichy Douches and many more. It was claimed that skin diseases, nervous debility, anaemia, glandular infections, all would benefit. To find out more about these treatments visit the Pump Room Museum where some of the weird paraphernalia can still be seen. With these treatments and the people who administered them, bath attendants, masseurs, doctors, everything was in place to make your stay uncomfortable but successful.

By 1912 there were 150,000 treatments annually. Newspapers wrote of the efficacy of the treatments and the joys of Harrogate and not just the local ones like the *Yorkshire Evening Post*. Newspapers as far away as *The Times of India*, *The Hot Lakes Chronicle and Rotorua Advertiser* in New Zealand and *The Brooklyn Daily Eagle* in the USA were recommending visits.

As the years went on and facilities developed, North Yorkshire was on the social map, part of 'The Season', a place where you could expect to bump into European royalty. Indeed in 1894 two of the granddaughters of Queen Victoria were to be seen racing their Bath chairs through the streets. It is a nice to think of Princess Alix of Hess having fun in Harrogate, for she became Empress of Russia and was shot with the rest of her family by the Bolsheviks in 1918.

Maharajahs, dukes, and cabinet ministers jostled with the likes of Clive of India, Sir Edward Elgar, Alfred Lord Tennyson and Charles Dickens. The latter was not so impressed with Harrogate as he wrote: 'the queerest place with the strangest people in it, leading the oddest lives.' Still Harrogate seemed to suit Agatha Christie when she went missing in 1926, and was eventually found staying in some style at The Swan.

The great days were over by the end of the Second World War and with the coming of the National Health Service in 1948 and free medicine for all, people would no longer pay for 'the cure'. In 1969 the Royal Baths closed for all treatments except the Turkish Baths.

***

The history of the Turkish bath in this country has had its up and downs. The Romans introduced us to the idea of sweating, not to keep clean but for 'sanitas' – health. The Dark Ages chose to forget about it. The Crusaders brought the idea back from the Holy Land; Henry VIII shut the 'stews' down. Seventeenth century travellers told tales of the

Turkish hammams and in London they became the place to go for a 'good time'! Victorian doctors made them respectable again.

Research for this little book has been thorough, though I have not felt the need to recreate private moments in the privy or to soap myself in a tin bath in front of my 'coal effect' electric fire. However, when invited, I was more than prepared to investigate the mysteries of the Turkish bath and to experience one of the treatments for which so many had flocked to Harrogate in the past and which can still be enjoyed to this day.

The Turkish Baths are in the Royal Baths Assembly Rooms, the small entrance belying the grandeur that lies within. Stepping from the bustling street you enter a Moorish fantasy of Islamic architecture: elegant arches lead through to richly tiled rooms with Italian terrazzo floors. At every step there are reclining couches besides small tables, inlaid with mother-of-pearl, inviting you to lie down and rest.

I carefully selected a ladies only afternoon and modestly took along my swimming costume – not feeling ready to bare all. The staff were kind and took me through the different stages. The deep silence of the steam room as the warmth penetrates aching bones and impurities drip from the body was followed by the agonising dip into a beautifully tiled cold plunge bath. Several elderly ladies in superb shape moved effortlessly between steam room and cold water. I gritted my teeth to avoid appearing 'sissy' but even I became used to the extremes of temperature and felt my circulation zinging. After that came the dry heat in the womb-like hot rooms lying on a slab, draped in a huge soft white towel, my head resting comfortably on a wooden block. Perfect peace, broken only by the rumbling of someone's stomach: a deeply cultured Harrogate voice apologised – the cause, an egg sandwich bolted for lunch.

Further sybaritic delights are available with sunbeds, massages by qualified staff and a whole range of beauty therapies. I emerged calm, refreshed, purified and ready for a slap-up tea up the road in Betty's Tea Rooms.

The magnificent Rest Room in the Harrogate Turkish Baths. (By kind permission of Harrogate Borough Council)

Upstairs in Harrogate Turkish Baths a 'Simplicitas' still going strong. (By kind permission of Harrogate Borough Council)

Cures for Constipation and Common Complaints

—— ᖇᗺ ——

'Bile Beans for biliousness and headache, indigestion, constipation, female weakness, dizziness, sallow complexions, pimples, impure blood and liver, stomach and bowel troubles. Price five shillings.'

Harrogate cures were not for everyone. For the ordinary North Yorkshire family living at the top end of the Dales, distances, poor communication and a certain frugality made you think twice before summoning a doctor. Before the introduction of penicillin in the 1940s and the coming of the National Health Service in 1948 there was little option but to cure yourself of common complaints.

North Yorkshire women faced with a minor illness in the family could be roughly divided into two categories: the 'just get on with it' brigade or the more compassionate ones who dabbled in homemade paste and potion. Either way you did not call the doctor out – that cost money. In the Yorkshire canon of medical self help the three benisons of rhubarb, goose grease and turnips cannot be underestimated, as will be revealed later in this chapter.

If none of these three were appropriate, a consultation of your 'commonplace book' would come up with a cure. Every self respecting housewife kept a 'commonplace' notebook of remedies, recipes and household hints handed down from mother to daughter, lovingly written out and increasingly dog eared over the years. Full of advice to deal with any emergency from 'a certain remedy for the cure of a mad

This advertisement still urges the people of York to a nightly dose of Bile Beans to keep them healthy, bright-eyed and slim.

dog' to the recipe for curing a bad back with vinegar and brown paper; the 'commonplace book' was a household fount of accumulated wisdom.

Eileen Crabtree of Ramsgill near Harrogate shared some of the secrets of her mother's 'commonplace book'. Her mother Mrs Ada Bennett had been trained as a cook but took a job at the Grand Hotel, Scarborough in the 1890s as a ladies' maid and looked after many theatrical artistes when they were appearing there for the season. Her favourites were Miss Sittwell and the Dare Sisters and for them she cleaned clothes and prepared salves for hands and whitener for necks and arms. There are 'receipts' for every emergency, including 'if gnats or earwigs get into the ear, a puff of tobacco smoke will render them helpless and afterwards the ears can be rinsed with a little warm water.' Later, as a mother, Mrs Bennett believed strongly in Turkey Rhubarb as a good purge and universal remedy.

North Yorkshire people were no different to the rest of the country in their belief that 'keeping regular' was the cornerstone of good

health. A self help book from the 1930s belonging to Heather Peacock
of Castle Bolton was very clear on the subject: 'nine-tenths of the evils
that flesh is heir to have their origin from "trouble in the interior", i.e.
imperfect digestion: ergo take care of the stomach. Avoid constipation
at all costs.' Not much doubt there.

Is it any wonder that constipation was such a universal problem as
long as there were outside privies? The public nature of many shared
privies, the sheer discomfort and the windy upward draught would
have clenched anyone's bowels. Everyone submitted to the weekly
purge.

Jean Day of Thornton Rust wrote that 'granny dosed her six
children weekly with senna tea.' Others used castor oil or a spoonful of
brimstone (another word for sulphur) and treacle on a Friday night.
Gregory Powder, a compound of rhubarb mixed with magnesia and
ginger was a favourite, so too was syrup of figs and often the day started
with a bowl of prunes. Some mothers made paper funnels and blew
sulphur powder down their children's throats and woe betide if you

*Commodious and superior this three-holer may be but is it any wonder that
constipation was a problem?*

blocked it with your tongue and the powder flew back into mother's face!

Alice Leneghan, one of a family of seven, wrote, 'Mother was a big believer in the weekly dose of liquorice powder given on a Friday night. The run down the garden to the "closet" was pretty hectic, with everybody desperate. Sometimes the waiting ended in an accident! In spring the dose was brimstone and treacle to clear our blood.'

Extra measures were taken in spring when it was considered necessary to have a 'good turn out' along with a general cleansing of the blood and system which had become 'sluggish' during the dark days and long nights of a Yorkshire winter. Irene Nicholson of Carperby furnished me with this little gem of a recipe favoured by her mother.

Mrs Keenlyside's Spring Medicine
Into a large jug place: 12 senna pods
2 teaspoons of Epsom Salts
Juice of a lemon
1 flat teaspoon of cream of tartar
Sugar to taste
Infuse the above in about 3 pints of boiling water, which has cooled
very slightly (in case the jug cracks).

Irene knows that it works as 'this was given to me and my father and each morning I had to drink a small glass of this infusion before leaving for school. I always hoped and prayed that the school bus did not break down – for obvious reasons!'

The coming of warmer days and lighter nights in North Yorkshire must have been greeted with mixed feelings. The Rites of Spring were celebrated in the Swaledale childhood home of Margaret Hobbs of Harmby Women's Institute with a whole arsenal of medicines. Sulphur and treacle as a tonic, Scotts Emulsion, cod liver oil and malt, syrup of figs needed or not, rhubarb either stewed or just the juice for cleansing the blood and if that did not do the trick – boiled nettles.

Young nettles made into a soup were a good source of iron during the Second World War. Your average Dalesman has never been at the cutting edge of alternative vegetarian food and often the soup had to be passed off as spinach, though many remained profoundly suspicious as to its true provenance.

For people used to a plain diet during the year a surfeit of rich food at Christmas could lead to an excess of all sorts of problems. Gwen Welton on the farm at Ellerbeck remembered one Christmas Eve. 'We always had "Frumenty" a kind of porridge made from pearl barley, cooked in milk with added sugar and nutmeg. One Christmas Eve my Father was extra hungry having just finished milking the cows by hand and he decided to have two helpings of Frumenty. Within an hour he was rolling on the floor with stomach pains caused by excess wind!'

Mrs Welton does not say whether he had any of 'Page Woodcock's Wind Pills' to hand, a well known remedy at that time; it is to be hoped so, for the Christmas food at Ellerbeck sounds rather good. 'On Christmas Eve we had ham sandwiches and cut the Christmas cake which we ate with Wensleydale cheese. Then on Christmas Day there would be goose with sage and onion stuffing followed by pudding. We had to bring a sprig of holly into the house on Christmas morning for luck and some of the village children would come "Lucky-birding".

'They would sing "Lucky bird, lucky bird,
>   Chuck, chuck, chuck,
>   Master an' missus, tahme ti' git up.
>   If you don't git up, ye'll have no luck.
>   Lucky bird, lucky bird,
>   Chuck, chuck, chuck."

Father had to give them coppers.' Let us hope that the effects of the Frumenty had subsided.

I approach the whole subject of wind delicately, not wishing to give offence to readers of a sensitive nature. However, it would be a very rare person indeed who could claim never to have suffered. I heard the following story at a group meeting of Women's Institutes at Crakehall where I was the speaker at a very jolly supper. It is a lesson for all those gentlemen who make no attempt to hold back when afflicted.

An old Yorkshire farmer had for many years suffered from strong and persistent wind which was at its worst and most offensive as he got out of bed in the morning. His wife used to complain about the strength and loudness of his problem saying, 'One day Jim, you'll fart so strongly that you'll blow your insides out.'

Jim took no notice until one Christmas morning his wife got up early to go down to the kitchen to see to the turkey. She crept out of bed leaving Jim still sleeping. As she was pulling out the gizzards from inside the turkey, she had an idea to teach Jim a lesson. Silently she crept upstairs and without waking Jim pulled back the waistband of his pyjama bottoms and placed the gizzards inside his pyjamas. She went back down to the kitchen and waited.

Ten minutes later she heard the most awful shouting and screaming followed by a loud bang of the bathroom door. Leaving him for a couple of minutes before going upstairs, the farmer's wife gently tapped on the bathroom door and innocently enquired, 'What on earth's the matter Jim?' A flustered and red faced Jim flung back the bathroom door saying, 'It was just as you said Mary, I've blown my insides out! – But, by the grace of God and these two fingers I've managed to get them back in again!'

***

The Christmas goose would have yielded lots of wonderful grease to be stored and used when illness struck. Ivy Dale as a child had her chest rubbed with goose grease and snuff, then brown paper placed onto the chest at night so that the grease would not get onto the bedclothes. 'I can remember it crackling as I tried to get to sleep.' Harold Hammond of Askrigg left me in no doubt as to the efficacy of goose grease, neglected now and with no place in modern medicine. As a butcher Harold had to withstand the cold and on a frosty morning he always rubbed goose grease onto his hands before going into the butcher's shop. If he ever caught a cold, goose grease rubbed onto the chest brought relief and for general aching joints there was nothing better.

When Harold started butchering in the 1950s everyone still had goose for Christmas. The village of Gayle with its wide stream was at one time well known for the number of geese kept by the villagers. Driving through the village needed extra vigilance because of the goose muck all over the road and woe betide anyone who skidded and hit one of those precious geese. In the early 1960s Harold would collect any unwanted goose grease and sell it on to two chemists in Skipton who made an ointment for joints. Valuable stuff at five pounds a jar.

As with goose grease, if it did you good, the smell of something was not going to put people off. Diane Bell of Thoralby Women's Institute remembered her mother advising that if she had a cold, sleeping with a

sweaty wollen sock round the neck would cure it. 'Chesty' children
seem to have suffered most at the hands of concerned mothers. A
rabbit skin or red flannel was regularly placed under a liberty bodice
and others had iodine lockets sewn into their clothes. One boy in
Askrigg used to go to school all muffled up against the cold with the
lockets sewn round the bottom of his shirt. Others were made to wear
little cotton bags impregnated with camphorated oil round their necks.
The redoubtable Mrs Bennett knitted 'vampers' which were body belts
saturated with the same aromatic substance. Schoolrooms must have
smelt to high heaven in the winter.

The mother of Eleanor Dinsdale of Carperby was a great believer in
the curative properties of turpentine. A dab of turpentine on a cut, two
drops on a lump of sugar for a chesty cough, and for backache a piece of
blanket, impregnated with turpentine and placed next to the skin
inside a corset. However, the smell that Eleanor always associated with
childhood was the cure that was always kept on the mantelpiece – a
mixture of olive oil and paraffin.

The Fawcetts were a loving and caring family whose home was a
byword for cleanliness and order but there was still something that cast
a dark shadow over Eleanor's childhood – nits! Eleanor had a beautiful
head of thick, blonde, curly hair which constantly attracted the little
beggars. No one else in the family was affected, just Eleanor, and her
mother worked long and hard to get rid of them. Eleanor's hair was
regularly annointed with the mixture from the mantelpiece and
wherever she went there was the waft of an unmistakable aura. Mother
combed frantically, Father would sit her on his lap and go through her
hair saying, 'Keep still, keep still – here's another one as big as a
donkey!'

Eleanor remarked that often people took the right thing but did not
know why. Honey was known to do you good, elderberry syrup or
homemade blackcurrant jam mixed with hot water helped a cold.
When Mary Bostock had a cold she was given brown sugar and butter
while others believed in keeping colds at bay with a daily dose of
Keppler's cod liver oil and malt.

Audrey Bailey as a child in the 1940s at Caldwell near Gilling was
treated regularly with the juice from turnips and as her parents grew
them on the farm there was never a shortage. After peeling you cut the
turnip into wedges and put them raw into a pie dish and covered them

with demerara sugar an inch thick and left to soak. A juice oozed from the turnip and you drained it off. This was good for coughs and bronchitis. Whooping cough was soothed with Golden Syrup in boiling water. Audrey was dosed with malt every day and if she did not want it there was none of this modern parent negotiation nonsense; her mother nipped her nose and down it would go.

All these sound very palatable but I would draw the line at the remedy for a sore throat or chest found in a little recipe book owned by Ruth Bridgewood of Ingleton. 'Finely shred 1 ounce of Mutton Suet, and allow to simmer in one pint of Milk for half an hour. Strain through muslin and drink while hot.' Ugh!

Ears could pose a problem to the brewer of home potions but even with this delicate organ the 'commonplace book' had an answer. Heather Peacock was made to hold a piece of toasted bread against her ear. Audrey Bailey's mother popped the middle of an onion into her own ear but gave Audrey a drop of almond oil on cotton wool. Eleanor Dinsdale's mother had the remedy for earache from Butcher Tom of Hawes which involved warming whisky in a spoon and dropping into the ear where there would be a great crackling noise as the wax dissolved.

For toothache I was impressed, but also horrified, by a remedy published in the *Wensleydale Advertiser* on 2nd January 1849. 'For agonising toothache when the patient is unwilling to submit to the radical cure of extraction. Gun cotton soaked in morphia dropped into the cavity and then filled with asbestos. The whole becomes solidified in a few seconds.' However, we do not need to take too seriously the other recommendaton for toothache. 'Two certain cures for toothache – either pulling out or driving further in!'

Finally even if you had none of these chronic illnesses but still felt a degree or so under there were patented tonics by the score. However, I shall pass on just one which Mary Bostock of Castle Bolton found in her mother's 'commonplace book'. 'A pick-me-up' consisting of: one bottle of rum, twelve fresh eggs (including eggshells), six lemons, one pound of honey, one pint of cream and one pound of demerara sugar. Let it stand for three days. Sip an eggcupful every morning while getting dressed. Not a bad way to start the day!

***

Life might have been harsh in North Yorkshire but a trip round the headstones of any country graveyard will show people who, in spite of everything, lived to a great age. It was hard to keep a large family fed, clothed, clean, decent and healthy, yet somehow the privies got cleaned, baths taken, clothes washed and children dosed. We can only salute those Yorkshire men and women who fought the good fight in their farmhouses and cottages against dirt and 'other filthy nuisances'.

Gone is the need for the weekly purge and our bowel movements have assumed their proper place in general health. Life in the lavatory and bathroom now is more serene and altogether sweeter. We acknowledge that we are not as tough as our forebears; hot water and strong flushes have robbed us of the steely resolve needed to use a garden privy or have a stripwash in a cold bedroom. We would not have it any other way for our bathrooms are warm, comfortable and above all private. What better room to keep just such a little book as this to read in those idle private moments and reflect on times past, behind the bathroom door.

One hundred and six years old! Proving that the fresh air and simple life of North Yorkshire can only do you good. (By kind permission of the Vicar of Askrigg, the Reverend Clive W. Malpass)

Acknowledgements

——— ⁊ ———

I would like to express my grateful thanks to everyone who took the trouble to help me with the writing of this book and especially to those who generously shared their memories and allowed me to take photographs.

A special mention must be made of Ann Holubecki for sharing her knowledge of the Dales and helping with the photographs.

The following people and organisations have been very helpful in my search for the sanitary past:

The Northern Echo
Darlington and Stockton Times
Craven Herald

The Dales Countryside Museum at Hawes
York City Archives Office
English Heritage at Mount Grace Priory near Thirsk

The Hon Harry Orde-Powlett, Bolton Castle in Wensleydale
The Newby Hall Estate at Ripon
The Chairman, Mr T. Gadsby, and Trustees of the H.W. Mawer Trust, Sion Hill Hall, Kirby Wiske near Thirsk

The staff at The Harrogate Turkish Baths, Harrogate
The Royal Pump Room Museum, Harrogate

North Yorkshire West Federation of Women's Institutes

My husband Ray who, as ever, has been unfailingly supportive in my quest for the privies, tin baths and washhouses of North Yorkshire.

Index

— ❧ —